FINDING A WAY OUT

Teens Write About Surviving Relationship Abuse

By Youth Communication

Edited by Laura Longhine

YOUTH COMMUNICATION

True Stories by Teens

FINDING A WAY OUT

EXECUTIVE EDITORS
Keith Hefner and Laura Longhine

CONTRIBUTING EDITORS
Nora McCarthy, Kendra Hurley, Rachel Blustain, Autumn Spanne,
Al Desetta, Sheila Feeney, and Philip Kay

LAYOUT & DESIGN
Efrain Reyes, Jr. and Jeff Faerber

COVER ART
Cezary Ladocha

ISBN 978-1-935552-21-5

Second, Expanded Edition

Printed in the United States of America

Youth Communication ®
New York, New York
www.youthcomm.org

Catalog Item #CW09-1

Table of Contents

If You Love Me, Don't Hit Me

> *Latonya urges a friend and all young women in
> abusive relationships to have the self-worth and self-
> confidence to get out.*

Blinded by Love?

> *The writer is beginning to realize that her boyfriend is
> abusive, but she can't bring herself to leave him.*

Black and Blue

> *Zoraida is only 12 when she starts going out with
> Tony, 19. Eventually he becomes so abusive that she
> seeks an order of protection.*

A Healing Connection

> *A clinical social worker explains how domestic violence
> affects women and how they can heal through therapy.*

Smarter Than That

> *Cheryl shares how her cousin, Renee, got into (and out
> of) a harrowing relationship.*

FICTION SPECIAL: Search for Safety

Using the Book

Introduction

Relationship abuse (also called domestic violence, dating abuse, or dating violence) is when one partner in an intimate relationship regularly uses a damaging behavior to control the other partner. Abuse can occur between a boyfriend and girl-friend or a married couple. It can occur in opposite sex and same sex relationships. The damage can be physical (hitting) or emotional, like when one partner is manipulative, threatening, or makes the other feel worthless.

In this book, teens write about witnessing relationship abuse in their families and experiencing it themselves. They describe how they escaped, and the steps they took to recover.

In Part I, teens write about growing up in violent homes. Parents may overlook the impact that witnessing domestic violence can have on their children. As Evaliz Andrades, a parent, writes: "Since [my husband] had not been physically abusive to the children, I felt they were safe." But as these writers show, watching a loved one fall victim to an abusive relationship can cause lasting emotional damage.

In "Tearing Our Family Apart," Jennifer Hoffman describes watching helplessly as her mother's abusive boyfriend takes over their lives. Her mother is unable to protect them. "She wouldn't stand up for me," Jennifer writes of one instance. "She had this empty look in her eyes like she wasn't in her body."

Jennifer becomes depressed and withdrawn, and eventually goes into foster care. Even after her mother finally leaves the boy-friend for good, Jennifer is overwhelmed with hurt and anger. It takes years of therapy to work through her feelings and rebuild a relationship with her mother.

How best to protect kids in violent homes is a question that many of these writers have wrestled with. Some teens, like Jennifer, don't seek help because they fear they'll be separated from the victimized parent. Others, like Princess Carr, are angry that the system didn't step in sooner to protect them and take them out of the home. Almost all of the teens describe trying desperately to protect the abused parent, even though they are helpless to do so. As Merli Desroiser and the author of "Turning Her In" discover, the best thing they can do is report the abuse and get help for themselves.

In Part II, teens write about being in abusive relationships themselves. They describe the warning signs, how to escape, and how therapy can help you recover and develop healthier relationships in the future.

Many of the writers describe relationships with males who seem caring and attentive at first, then become more and more possessive and controlling, then violent. As the author of "Breaking Free" writes:

"At first he would just ask me to do things...and I would because I cared for him so much. I thought doing things your man wanted was what love was about. But after a while, he became more demanding."

As their partners grow increasingly violent, many of the writers describe feeling trapped. They become convinced that they must have caused the abuse somehow, and sometimes feel pity for the abusive partner. They are afraid of being alone and of what might happen if they try to leave. As Zoraida Medina writes:

"I truly hated Tony by this point, but I also felt stuck with him. So I learned how to act in ways that wouldn't upset him as much. I acted as if I had no friends, as if the world I was living in was over, and the more I acted like this, the more I started believing it. I felt so ashamed all the time."

In "Putting Up With Her Hands," Derrick B. shows that men can be victims of relationship violence, too. As a child, he is physically and emotionally abused by his mother. When he finds a girl who treats him well and believes in his better self, he is so hooked that he can't let her go, even after she starts hitting him.

In "A Healing Connection" a therapist explains why it's difficult to escape an abusive relationship, and how counseling can not only help you leave, but also strengthen your ability to find better relationships in the future.

Violent relationships can have devastating effects on your life, your sense of self, and your other relationships. But as these stories show, you can recover.

In the following stories, names have been changed: *Turning Her In; Breaking Free; If You Love Me, Don't Hit Me; Blinded By Love?;* and *Smarter Than That.*

Note to Readers: Survival Strategies

When you read this book, it can be hard not to focus on the abuse and victimization suffered by the writers. But don't let that overwhelm you. If you read the stories closely, one thing you'll see is the amazing things these young writers did to keep themselves safe. Escaping a violent home or an abusive relationship is difficult, and leaving can take a long time. But these brave writers never gave up. Here is just a partial list of all the ways they coped with their pain and reached out for help.

(Note: Many of these teens tried desperately to change the abuser and stop the abuse. But they found that didn't work. If you or a parent is in an abusive relationship, the best thing you can do is protect yourself and escape as soon as you can).

Writers who survived violent homes:

Tell my mom what's happening
Pray
Threaten to call the cops
Go to family therapy
Tell my mom to leave
Talk to my school therapist
Tell my mom how I feel
Write poetry
Make collages
Run away

File a police report
Go into foster care
Distance myself from my dad
Leave the house during fights
Spend time at a friend's house
Graduate high school
Tell other family members
Tell a trusted social worker
Tell child welfare
Connect with a foster family

Writers who survived abusive relationships:

Persuade partner to go to rehab
Leave to stay with family
Go to a couples counselor who
  confronts the abuser
File a police report
Move to a new home
Join an advocacy group for
  survivors
Go back to school
Try to stand up for myself
Tell my coach
Tell a friend
Tell my social worker
Move into a foster home

Stop speaking to my abusive
  boyfriend
Get an order of protection
Press charges against him
Learn more about abusive
  relationships
Realize the abuse is not my fault
Move back into my mom's
  house
Get support from other family
  members
Testify against my abuser
Call the police
Stop taking his calls
Stay with a family member in
  another state

PART I: Violence at Home

Tearing Our Family Apart

By Jennifer Hoffman

Growing up, I didn't have a perfect family, but all of us were happy. My mom never actually said she loved us but she was always there and gave us what we needed. She signed us up for sports, came to our open houses, and took us to Chuck E. Cheese's when we got our report cards.

But things changed when I turned 10. My mom ran into an old acquaintance and he came over to our house the same day. They immediately started dating.

The beginning of their relationship was like a fairy tale. He was the dad I had always wanted. He had kids of his own, and it seemed like he was always making them laugh and giving them hugs. He set rules for them that were really strict but I assumed it was because he was worried about them. He made us feel like part of his family by taking us out to dinner and the movies. It felt right.

But after a few months my mom started to change. She didn't go out as much. She made up excuses to avoid taking my younger sister and me to our sports and Girl Scouts. She said, "You guys don't need to go anyway."

Soon we weren't allowed to go anywhere with my mom, unless he was with us. He would tell us straight up, "You're not going because I said so." He wanted my mom to be home as much as possible. When she went out with him, she wasn't allowed to even look at other guys.

He put her down and made her feel bad about herself. If my mom joked around about leaving him, he'd get serious and say, "You know you need me," or, "No one else will want you, you're nothing."

After they had been together about six months, I saw my mom crying one night. It was the first time I'd seen her cry. She told us that he'd slapped her. By this time, I had also seen him whip his kids with a belt and slap them on the face.

I felt so badly for my mom. I felt like it was my fault because I couldn't do anything to stop it. I wondered, "Why is he doing this?"

Instead of breaking up with him, my mom decided we should move in with him. He was very controlling. He made my mom cut her hair short like a man and wear really short dresses. She had hickies on her neck that looked like dog bites.

It seemed like my mom chose him over us. One time he told me to clean the kitchen, but I didn't hear what he said. When I asked again he whipped me with a belt and threw a chair on me.

Later that night I told him, "You can't hit me because you don't have permission." I looked over at my mom and asked her if she had given him permission, but she wouldn't stand up for me. She had this empty look in her eyes like she wasn't in her body.

I tried all kinds of things to get us away from him. Some nights I prayed to God for him to go away, but God never answered my prayers. I threatened to call the cops, but I was too scared that they'd take us away from my mom.

One day I packed my stuff in a little kid suitcase and asked my little sister to run away with me. I said that we would go find our dad. But she was too young and too scared to actually go, and I was afraid to leave my mom. I didn't want her to be alone.

I told my mom that she needed to break up with him, that what he was doing was wrong. She'd say, "But he loves me" or, "We care about each other."

At school I slowly stopped talking to my friends and started hanging out in the bathroom stalls. At recess, I hung out by myself and collected rocks instead of playing tetherball. I didn't want to be accepted by anyone because I was feeling bad about myself.

My mom wouldn't stand up for me. She had this empty look in her eyes like she wasn't in her body.

My mom saw that I was having problems so she signed me up for therapy, and my therapist got her to come to family therapy. We talked about how he was tearing our family apart. Friends and family had been telling my mom she needed to break up with him. It all finally got to her.

One day, eight months after they met, she told us, "I broke up with him." I was happy, but I didn't know how to express it. My family doesn't talk when bad things happen, so we just moved out and acted like the family was OK again.

After about two months, my mom started going to "the store" for three hours and wouldn't let us go with her. I got suspicious. I yelled and asked her again and again, "You're back with him, aren't you?" She finally admitted that she was. I felt like dying.

They were off and on for the next two years. She would break up with him and we'd all think it was over. A few weeks later she'd be back with him, sneaking around because she knew I'd be angry.

When I found out, I'd give her the usual lecture. I'd tell her that he wasn't the right person for her and she was being brainwashed. She would look at me like she knew it was the truth, but she was stuck.

My mind was always on my mom. After school I went to a day treatment center where I did art therapy to work on my anger. I was also put on medication. But at school I didn't feel like I fit in. I would ditch class and use my bus pass to go around the city. Eventually I stopped going to school altogether. I started eating a lot. I would only leave the house once a week to go to the store.

When he came to the house I'd cuss him out, so he stopped coming inside. He would knock on the door and wait for my mom in the car. I hated his guts and I called him "psychopathic idiot." I even made up a song about it and sang it really loud when my mom was on the phone with him.

That November, my mom told him she wanted to break up with him, then didn't come home. I stayed up all night waiting for her. I was so scared. I believed he would have killed her just so no one else could have her.

When she finally got back, she told me he had kidnapped her. She had a big knot on her forehead, and later she admitted that he had head-butted her. She took pictures to show the cops to get a restraining order, but within two weeks she was with him again.

*I*n March, I was placed in foster care because I hadn't been going to school. I was put in a group home with five other girls. I was so depressed, I didn't even care about leaving my family.

Two months later, on my 13th birthday, my mom told me she'd broken up with him for good. I figured she was going to get back with him. But she didn't.

Even though he was gone, my pain wasn't. I had shoved the hurt down for so long that it had caused a huge chain reaction. I didn't know who I was anymore.

His always threatening to hit us made me afraid and intimidated by other people. I had never felt so much anger, hurt, and humiliation. I didn't see the world as a happy place anymore. I didn't like myself and I didn't think I could ever be happy again.

When I went home on weekends I would scream and yell at my mom, "It's your fault I'm in the group home!" I wanted to make her feel guilty. He was gone and I had no one else to take my anger out on.

I threatened to call the cops, but I was too scared that they'd take us away from my mom.

In 8th grade, with the help of my school therapist, I talked about it with my mom for the first time without her saying, "Get over it." I talked about how it made me feel. She looked like she was about to cry, but she didn't apologize. She never has. She said he was controlling her and it wasn't her fault.

It took another two years of therapy to finally get over being angry at my mom. Our relationship is better now. I can have a conversation with her without bringing him up. Through therapy I realized that even though he treated her badly, she was used to it because her dad was also abusive. My mom didn't know what a healthy relationship was.

This experience has stained me. I don't smile very often and I prefer to be by myself. I'm not good at expressing my emotions. I still have a lot of unanswered questions, like, "Why did this happen to me?"

It was a long struggle staying in school, but I made it! I graduated in August and plan to attend college. I want to be a psychologist or a lawyer. Now that I'm emancipated from the foster care system, I feel a lot more free. But at times I worry that history will repeat itself, that someone will hurt me and I'll stop doing everything in my life that means something to me.

Finding a Way Out

I'm trying to stay positive. When I'm angry with other people, I write poetry and make collages about the pain I feel. But sometimes I think the anger inside will never go away. It amazes and depresses me at the same time to know that so much pain could be caused by one person.

Jennifer wrote this story for LA Youth, a newspaper by and for teens in California. Copyright © LA Youth. Reprinted with permission.

Karolina Zaniesienko

Leaving the Bastard

By Merli Desrosier

It was a mild fall night. My boyfriend and I were on the phone talking about how we hadn't seen each other for a while. Our hormones were racing. "I'm alone. I wish you were here," I said, though really I thought it was too late. My boyfriend thought differently. He said he would be there in 15 minutes so I should keep a lookout.

I had to ask myself if it was worth it, knowing how mad my father would be if he found me with a boy. But I assured myself that my father wouldn't come home till morning.

When my boyfriend arrived, he was all over me, and our clothes began to disappear. We were in the heat of passion when I heard the door click. My heart jumped and then so did I. I went to the door and spoke to my father as nicely as I could. He asked me what was going on and I said, "Nothing." Then he came in and saw my boyfriend.

I saw fear in my boyfriend's eyes. He didn't know what to do or where to go and neither did I. My father turned off the light and locked the door. Then he took a metal pole and lunged at my boyfriend with it, but I jumped in front. I really don't know what gave me the strength. I just knew I wasn't going to let my father hurt the one person I loved.

He tried again and I jumped between them again. Then my father told my boyfriend to get out.

"Don't do anything to her, mister," my boyfriend said.

"I'll do anything I want, now get out," my father replied and slammed the door. Then he turned to me. He pulled up my nightgown and saw I had nothing underneath.

"What's this?" he said. I pulled away but punches started hitting my head, over and over, like water from the shower head.

To this very minute I wonder: If she had left, would she still be alive?

I could only think, "This man might try to put me in the hospital. I need to get away." I made a dash for the door. I didn't care that I had on nothing but my nightgown because my life was at stake.

My father tried to grab my neck, covering my bare flesh with his bear-like hands, but I escaped. I ran into the hall and began to yell, hoping somebody would hear me. My father grabbed me and began punching my head again. Somebody finally opened the door and my father tried to pull me into the house. With all my strength and fear I pulled myself from him and ran to the neighbor's door. My father went downstairs. I stood there in the middle of the hallway with blood covering my nightgown and realized my night of fun had turned into a night of terror.

I ran back inside the apartment and put some clothes on. I was determined to do what I wish my mother had done when she was alive: leave the bastard.

When I was growing up, my father was rarely there. When he did come around—usually once a week—he would beat my mother. Sometimes he would wake us so we could see him holding a knife right under her neck. The most painful memory was the time he took a metal rod and hit her over the head, which caused her to go unconscious. I thought he'd killed her, and then he threw me on her lifeless-looking body.

Another time, I heard my mother scream from her bedroom, and it wasn't sounds of pleasure. She was telling my father to get away. The bastard wouldn't leave her alone. Instead, he raped her.

My mother was ill with sickle cell anemia, and was often in pain. She never understood why my father would want to inflict more pain on her. I don't understand it either.

My mother was a good person and could always get the best out of me. We used to go out together and shop, and people thought she was my sister. In the house we'd play hand games and make up stories; she was a writer just like me. My mother didn't act like an authority to me, she was more like a best friend. She was a wonderful mother and didn't deserve the hard life she lived. In 1993, my mother died of sickle cell, but I believe the stress from my father helped to kill her. I've asked myself so many times, "Why couldn't the bastard just die and let my mother live?"

Watching my father abuse my mother was terrible. I was helpless. I could do nothing but watch, tell him that I hated him, cry, and help my mommy heal once he was gone. When my mother talked to me about my father, she'd say, "I don't know what to do. I want to leave but I can't. I have nowhere to go. He was so nice to me when we first met, then suddenly that good man died. I was left to fight the devil and I don't know if I will be able to fight him long."

One thing I don't understand is why she never got away. On one occasion, my mother told me to pack up my things and I did, but we never left. That hurt because my mother was hurt.

To this day I don't know—was there really nowhere to go? Or was she afraid to go? Why didn't she have him arrested? Was she afraid to have him arrested? Or did part of her love him? To this very minute I wonder: If she had left, would she still be alive?

The night my father turned his violence on me, I tiptoed down the stairs of my four-story building and pondered what would become of me. While I was on my way down, my father came back in. I was terrified, but I hid in the corner and he passed me by. Once I was outside, I saw the police rounding the corner. Somebody had called them for me. When they saw my tear-stained face, they knew who I was, which was good, because I was so choked up I could hardly speak.

My father came downstairs and saw me and the police, and knew he was facing a world of trouble. I couldn't even look at him—it made me too sick to think that the same thing that happened to my mother had just happened to me. As I stood there, I didn't know what in the world to do, so at first all I did was cry and try to sort out my feelings. The way I reacted, I realized, might dictate what would become of my brother, my sister, and me.

The police asked if I wanted my father arrested. I did, but I was worried that saying yes wouldn't be right. I wasn't the only one who would be affected. I had to think about where my brother and sister would go. I knew they might go into foster care and I didn't feel they should have to.

Someone began whispering in my ear and I knew exactly who it was, it was my mother's spirit. "Let God handle it, my baby, He'll handle it," she told me. That's what she'd said when she was alive, and for that moment I listened to her. As I slowly drifted back to earth I knew I couldn't tell the police to arrest my father.

The police officer asked me a second time if I wanted my father arrested, and I said, "No." But as soon as I did, I felt so mad at myself for not letting my words be heard. I had the opportunity to send a message across to him that violence is not the way to communicate, and I was choosing not to.

Then the cop asked me to write a police report so that if there was another incident with my father, they would have this complaint on file. At first I believed that they would just file away what I said. But as I stood there with the breeze hitting my face, remembering exactly what he'd done to me, I began to realize that my father hitting me with his closed fist wasn't right, that it wasn't right to choke me either, and that doing those things was also illegal. As I wrote down what had happened I knew that my father would probably go to jail.

And then, somehow, that was OK with me. All the other issues—my sister and brother, what other people would say—just went out of my mind. If someone asked me if I cared, I would have said no, because he deserved it. It was his turn to suffer.

As I put the police report into the officer's hand, I could see the expression of a man who would never do such things to his own child. Then the words came out of his mouth, slow but clear. "I'm sorry to say this, but your father has committed assault in the third degree and he has to be arrested."

When the officer said that, it was like a burden being lifted from my shoulders. My father would be punished and all I'd had to do was write down exactly what he did. The way I saw it, his own action would really be what got him arrested, and that brought a smile on the inside of me.

After I gave the report to the police, I didn't know what happened to my father because I went to stay with relatives, and then after a year I went into foster care. I did learn that within weeks, my dad was out of jail and back with my brother and sister because they said they wanted to go back home.

I don't know if this is the best for them because my father is hardly home to take care of them and he doesn't give them enough love. (When I see them, I try to give them the love a parent should.) But I don't think they're in any danger, either. When he's home, they just have to make sure he can find his remote control and they're fine.

When my brother was younger, occasionally my dad would beat him. But now my brother's less afraid, in part because I had my father arrested. We know there are options if we get hit.

I hope that getting arrested taught my dad a lesson, though sometimes I think that if he had been in jail longer he would have learned his lesson better. Though I say that, I also chose not to press charges. I just wasn't ready to go that far. People often say that until abusive men are really punished for beating their wives and kids, too many of them will never stop. But when it comes to tearing up your own family, sometimes pressing charges just feels like the wrong thing to do. At least having him arrested gave him a little idea that it is wrong to

It made me sick to think that the same thing that happened to my mother had just happened to me.

put his hands on another human being, and that makes me feel good.

I feel the world takes it lightly that women get abused. I don't know whose responsibility it is to change that—whether abused women need to change themselves or whether there needs to be more help for them and for abusive men, too. As I get older, I hope to learn more about domestic violence and find ways to defend women in the same situation my mother was in.

Sometimes girls who grow up in abusive homes turn around and get into abusive relationships themselves. But watching my mother being beaten by my father set in my mind at a young age that no man would ever put his hands on me and get away with it. I've made sure that with my own relationship, I have total communication and that I take time and space to get to know the guys I'm with. That makes me feel safe.

It has been one and a half years since that night. It's hard to believe that I can look back and say that a lot of good came out of it. Sometimes it takes something extreme, like having your father arrested, to change the situation you're in.

Merli was 17 when she wrote this story. She later graduated from college and continues to advocate for youth in foster care.

Elizabeth Deegan

Take Us Away

By Princess Carr

When I hear the words domestic violence, I remember hearing my mother screaming for help in the middle of the night. I remember taking a washcloth and wiping down her swollen face after her boyfriend (a cop) had decided that she did not make breakfast the exact way he wanted it. I remember being as young as 5 and hiding with one of my younger brothers and praying to God that she'd do either one of two things: shut up or fight back. At times I used to block out the sound of her tears and daydream about someone coming into my scary real world to lift me out and make it all better.

For 12 years I watched my mother being abused. I felt torn between feeling sorry for her and hating her because I felt she was supposed to be stronger than that. I also wanted to protect her, and I felt inadequate because I knew that I was not big enough or strong enough to stop him. I've gone through a lot in my life, including being abused myself, but watching my mother being hurt is the worst thing I've ever gone through.

When the state got wind of what was going on in our house and wanted to move my brothers and me, my mother believed they were only trying to hurt her. You see, we were her life, and without us she felt lost. But she also decided that without her boyfriend, she'd be lost too. And since she made the choice to keep on loving him, even with the abuse, she also made the choice that we, her children, had to deal with it. I know she was in pain, but I also believe she was selfish. I don't believe she ever really considered the effects her choices would have on us.

Right now you're probably saying to yourself, "Well why couldn't the state find a way to get her help and leave her children with her?" I'm sure that there are times when that works, but in my case, that kind of help was not enough.

You see, when I was about 6, my mother finally did accept help from child welfare. They moved us into a shelter for single mothers and children. The shelter wasn't all that bad. For the most part, the people were nice. The school I went to was OK and as far as I knew, everything was going back to the way it should have been. No more screaming in the night. My brothers and

Watching my mother being hurt is the worst thing I've ever gone through.

I weren't so scared and my mommy was smiling again. Proves your point? That if the state gives mothers a chance, everything will be all right?

Well, after a few months, my mother took our newfound peace and threw it all away. She moved her boyfriend back into our life and into our shelter rooms. (He wasn't supposed to be there, but it was a big shelter and nobody checked.) I don't think it ever occurred to my mom that we were doing better as individuals and as a family without him. I don't know if she even noticed that our nightmares (hers included) were coming less and less, that we could laugh more freely and that generally we felt safer.

I keep saying "I don't think" but what I mean to say is that I hope it never occurred to her, because if it did, that would really be the biggest betrayal. Her actions have left me scarred. I'm 21, and I still feel such a fear of an unexpected attack that I always double-check my doors and windows to make sure they're locked. Sometimes I have nightmares and wake up crying. And I don't think I will ever be able to hear the words "I'm sorry" without feeling angry that they might be insincere.

I entered foster care after I ran away, but I wish they had taken me away when they first found out about the abuse. I'm not saying that's always the right move. Sometimes children end up in even worse situations.

But I do believe, and I feel no remorse in saying, that many times it takes having their children removed from them—whether for a long time or temporarily—for mothers to realize that their children need to come before the abusive relationships they're in.

Princess was 21 when she wrote this story.

Cezary Ladocha

How I Escaped: A Parent's Perspective

By Evaliz Andrades

I started dating him when I was 16. Within two weeks he told me he loved me. I was flattered but felt he was a bit too obsessive, so after a few weeks, I broke it off.

I remember that day clearly. After I told him we were over, I got into a taxi and he ran after the taxi screaming that he loved me. I felt so guilty.

For weeks after that he stalked me. He would show up at my house at all hours of the day looking for me. My mother was concerned. She found his behavior dangerous and, over the next two years, tried to break us apart. But I thought he must really love me to pursue me like that. I felt almost obligated to be with him.

When I was 18 I moved in with him. Then he asked me to marry him, but I had this feeling inside that I shouldn't so I refused. Around that time, I found myself feeling empty spiritually. I was longing for a God who was up close and personal. On March 13, 1988, I had the personal encounter with God I was longing for—I became a born again Christian.

Converting gave me a deep desire to make things right before my God. I believed it was my duty as a Christian woman to be married to the man I was living with. I felt torn, but a week after my conversion, I got married.

A few months into our marriage, my husband started using crack cocaine. It got so bad his own mother told me to leave him.

As a young wife, I felt like he did not love me enough to stay clean and sober. I felt rejected. At other times, I wondered if I had failed him in any way. I fasted for him and many nights I stayed up praying, in tears, asking God to bring my husband home safe. I believed God could save him, change him, cleanse him, free him from this addiction.

Eventually, with the help of my pastor, I was able to persuade him to go to a Christian rehab. He converted and became clean and sober. Six months later he came back a new man, or so I thought.

I kept trying to save him, believing that if only I loved him, surely he would change. But he didn't.

We began to grow in our faith and in our involvement with the church. Two years later we conceived. I was so happy. I would often look at my belly in the mirror and pose, loving the changes that were taking place in my body, heart, and mind.

Unfortunately, instead of feeling closer to me, my husband rejected me. He became emotionally abusive. He also got involved with drugs again. During one of the most important and vulnerable seasons of my life, I was all alone.

This time his drug use was so bad we lost our apartment. Pregnant and homeless, I stayed with my grandmother in Puerto Rico for several months until he got help from the church and got clean again. I felt it was my duty to forgive him and give him a chance.

My husband seemed broken and remorseful. I later realized that he was sorry for what he had lost, not sorry for what he had done, two very different things.

As the years progressed, he became angrier and angrier. When I crossed him, especially by taking a part-time job and returning to school, he would intimidate and threaten me. The more I asserted myself, the more out of control he felt, the angrier he got.

He would get in my face in menacing ways, wetting my face with his saliva from all the yelling, and blocking me from leaving the room with his body. He would break my things and throw stuff at me, later saying he only threw things in my direction. One time he took my precious figurine collection and smashed it up.

He also humiliated me in public, screaming at me in church, in the supermarket, and even at my job. Co-workers and some friends and neighbors started to make comments to me about how he treated me, and I wished they would confront him about his behavior, but no one did. That reinforced my feeling that I was responsible for him.

I also made excuses for him. In my quest to understand him, analyzing his childhood and disappointments in life, I kept myself in a hole. I kept trying to save him, believing that if only I loved him, surely he would change. But he didn't.

I sometimes thought about divorcing him, but I feared that might be unbearable for my kids and myself. Besides my church family, I had no family support in the United States. I felt trapped, emotionally, physically, and spiritually. I was a young woman with a part-time job, no college education, and young children to support.

I also didn't want my children to grow up without their father. I grew up without a father and it hurt. And since he had not been physically abusive to the children, I felt they were safe.

At times, my husband prayed and promised to change. We had what I called "honeymoon periods." After a big fight, I would say I was going to leave him, and he would become a teddy bear full of remorse, begging me to stay. We had getaways, minivacations.

Then we would go to counseling with my pastors and church elders and I would dare to dream again. I didn't want to believe that my God could not fix this situation. Faith was my way of coping with despair. Of course, the honeymoon would only last a few months. He refused to go beyond the step of acknowledging his "anger problem" to doing something about it.

Eventually we got couples counseling with a psychologist who called it like it was, confronting my husband about his abusive behavior. After witnessing one of my husband's episodes, the psychologist told him, "If I were her, I would not care to live with you either."

Seeing a doctor confront my husband about his abusive behavior, I started feeling less trapped and more sure of myself. I stopped wondering if I was exaggerating.

Unfortunately, that same year I became pregnant with our third child. Although I felt certain I needed to leave, I was soon on bed rest and dependent on my husband.

Then, when I was six months pregnant, I found out my husband was having an affair. I was deeply hurt and felt great shame. It was as if everything I had endured came to naught.

When I confronted him, he started to scream at me, denying the whole thing. Then he put his hands around my neck and choked me. As I struggled to get away, I looked at him in shock, and he let go of me. Amidst tears I kept saying, "I can't believe you choked me."

I immediately filed a police report, but the cops said since there was no evidence, they couldn't make him go. He refused to leave. I believed I had nowhere to go with my two little girls, so I stayed under the same roof with him.

Finally, after two more incidents, my neighbors called the police, and three days before I gave birth, they made him leave permanently. I am so glad that I was able to stay in our home with my children, and he was forced to leave.

Between caring for a newborn, raising two little girls, and dealing with eviction notices (because I could not pay our rent), I was truly overwhelmed for the next few months.

I drank my tears daily. The pain would hit me like a wave. I would be walking down the street and suddenly a memory of him, of us, would hit me, and I would feel like just sitting on the curb and crying. I would be on the bus and a small tear would slip down my face, escaping my sunglasses.

The nights were especially hard. As soon as it got dark outside, a shadow of sadness would come over me as well. I would call upon my few close friends for prayer. The Bible kept me sane. Scriptures, like the one that says, "This too shall pass," gave me incredible hope.

I would say I was going to leave him, and he would become a teddy bear full of remorse, begging me to stay.

My children were a comfort to me as well. Once my 6-year-old looked me in the eye and said, "It's OK, Mommy, we could still be a happy family without Daddy." This touched me profoundly.

It's been five years since I left my ex-husband. Now, as I look back, it all seems like a bad dream. Despite the financial cost, and the grief I felt when my marriage ended, getting out of that relationship has been only positive for me. The children seem to be adapting well. It has not been an easy road for them, but they are resilient.

I got help from several programs. Section 8 helped me with the rent and the money to relocate, giving us a brand new start. Joining Voices of Women, an organization of domestic violence survivors, gave me community. Counseling and advocacy helped me understand the dynamics of domestic violence and deal with the guilt laid upon me for years. I came to believe that I was not put on this earth to serve as anyone's doormat, or to be drained emotionally by someone's abusive behavior.

School also became a tool of healing. Pursuing an education was a dream of mine I used to weep about in prayer, a secret desire I dared not share for fear of being ridiculed. But I've finished my bachelor's degree and am now pursuing a Master's in Social Work at Columbia University.

By the grace of God, today I am a new woman, continuing to heal daily. The same hope I once invested in my marriage, I now invest in my own life. I've turned my hope towards me.

Evaliz wrote this story as a member of The Voices of Women Organizing Project (VOW), which trains domestic violence survivors to advocate for change. This story was published in Rise, a magazine by and for parents with children involved in the child welfare system. www.risemagazine.org

Byron Pabon

Can Men Who Batter Stop?
Two perspectives on treatment

Reporting by Cynthia Orbes

The idea of "treating" domestic violence offenders is relatively new, and there's a lot of debate about it. Can men who batter women really change? And if so, what's the best way to get them to do that? While all court-mandated programs have to meet certain guidelines, some programs take a hard-line approach, emphasizing that men who batter are choosing to do something wrong and need to take responsibility for that. Other programs are more therapeutic, with an added focus on helping men figure out for themselves why they've been battering and how they can stop. We spoke with Vicki Gorder and Ted Bunch, who run two different treatment programs, to find out more.

Creating a Desire for Change
Interview with Vicki Gorder

Partners in Change is a counseling agency in Colorado Springs. We do all different types of counseling, but we specialize in domestic violence offender treatment and drug and alcohol counseling. Domestic violence offenders can join our program voluntarily, but most of them are sent here by the courts.

There are state goals and curricula that we have to follow, and there's a lot of stress on accountability and education. But I'm from the camp that believes that for long-term change to occur, you also have to engage these men in a therapeutic relationship.

You can say, "This is bad, this is wrong, and if you do it again you're going to go to jail," and people may say "OK," but the minute they get out of there, they're gonna do what they're gonna do. I believe that to see long-term change, I have to hold these men accountable but also create an environment where men want to change—not because I say it's wrong, but because they do.

I have to create an environment where men want to change— not because I say it's wrong, but because they do.

Part of my approach is creating the desire to change. Most men (although not all) truly want to be a man of honor and integrity. I ask them, "What is your own sense of honor telling you?" Most men are taught not to hit women, so they're violating their own beliefs, not just mine.

A lot of my clients have never thought of it that way. They're used to being told, "You're a batterer, a bad person." All the defense mechanisms kick in and they want to minimize their behavior and shift the blame. They say, "It wasn't that wrong. It's not like we're Ike and Tina." I say, "Well, how wrong do you see it as being? How wrong was it for you?" Often they've come from a violent home, so the fact that they punched a hole in the wall doesn't seem that bad, because they didn't punch their partner. Sometimes they think they're handling their anger well.

I also tell my clients, "We all do things for a reason. You use violence because there's a payoff—it gets someone else to do what you want. But what does it cost you?" For a lot of men, when they start to look at what kind of role model they're being for their children, that's the avenue of change. They want their sons to look up to them, and they don't want their daughters to end up getting beaten.

Domestic violence treatment for offenders is still relatively new. There's a lot of controversy around what does and doesn't work, and the idea that we'll find this one solution to fix offenders is not reality. They have potential and it's up to us to help them change. We haven't perfected that yet.

There are men who have been to treatment who are not going to change. But I don't believe that's the majority. Most men who are working to change will say they feel better about themselves and have a different type of relationship with their partners—one that's loving, warm, and nurturing. They begin to get what they really wanted.

These men want relationships, but they don't know how to get their needs met without using violence. When they learn how to earn respect, admiration, and love, they realize the difference between love and fear. Love is very different from compliance that they've forced out of their partner by using violence.

Vicki Gorder is the co-director of Partners in Change,
an offender treatment program in Colorado Springs.

Teaching Respect
Interview with Ted Bunch

At Safe Horizon, the program that deals with offenders is the domestic violence accountability program. Offenders who've been arrested for domestic violence get sent here by the court. It's actually not counseling—it's education and it's about holding men accountable.

Our perspective is that men don't need therapy, that they know how to be respectful and non-abusive, but they choose not to. We know that because an abusive man goes through the rest of his life without being abusive.

I think that men need to be re-educated. Domestic violence is a learned behavior that can be unlearned. Counseling has nothing to do with that. It's about education.

> *I think that men need to be re-educated. Domestic violence is a learned behavior that can be unlearned.*

In our classes, we teach the dynamics of power control and what domestic violence is, that it's not just physical. We also provide education around a number of other topics like the history of violence against women, the effects of domestic violence on children, and how domestic violence is similar to other kinds of oppression, like racism and homophobia. It's just a different group being the dominant power.

Hopefully we inform men that their behavior is something that they can change right now. They're acting out what they've been taught by society.

Individually, to stop battering, men need to take personal responsibility and make changes in their life. But we believe that domestic violence is not really an individual ill, it's a social ill, the same way as if someone is racist. How we can help him stop as a society is to accept that men have been taught to view women in certain ways, and that we have to teach gender equality so that women are respected in the same way men are. More importantly, other men have to speak out and say that this is wrong.

Men who have been through batterers programs re-offend at about the same rate as men who haven't had any treatment at all, so batterers programs are not the cure. And just because a man doesn't get arrested again doesn't mean he doesn't do it again.

Every man is capable of changing. There's no doubt in my mind. I know they're capable of being respectful, because these men are respectful to other people in their lives. When he's angry with his boss or his friends, he doesn't take it out on them, he takes it out on her. It's about choice.

But I don't think that a woman's life is any safer because a man has been through a batterers program. We tell women whose partners are sent here that when he comes back, she should plan for the man she knows him to be, and not the one she hopes him to be.

Ted Bunch is the senior program director for the Domestic Violence Accountability Program at Safe Horizon, an organization in New York City that seeks to prevent violence and support victims of crime and abuse.

Ora Obhas

Dad Done Us Wrong

By Anonymous

When I was a little girl, my daddy would go hang out with his friends after a hard day's work and I would wait up for him. When I finally heard his key turn in the lock, I would run to greet him with a hug. Then I would tell him about all the wonderful things that had happened while he was gone. When I was finished he would tell me about his friends, and if a holiday was coming up, what he was planning on getting Mommy. I was his confidante, and when he was gone, his eyes and ears.

My Daddy always picked me up every afternoon from day care. But one day, I walked out to his blue station wagon and there was a woman sitting in the front seat—my seat. She was light-skinned, and she had dark brown hair with ugly blond highlights.

"Who the hell is she?" I thought. "Why is she in my Daddy's

front seat?"

When we finally dropped her off, the ugly lady actually turned and gave my daddy a kiss on the lips! Only my mommy gave my daddy kisses like that. "Who was that lady?" I asked him when we drove off. No answer. "Daddy, who was that lady?" Still no answer.

"Daddy had this woman in the car, Mommy," I blurted out as soon as we got home. Nobody was going to make me sit in the back seat to make room for some ugly lady I didn't even know.

"What woman? Did you know her?"

"No."

"You sure it wasn't one of your aunts or something?"

"No."

My father must have known that I was going to tell, because when my mother went into the bedroom to question him about it, she found him fast asleep. Pretending to sleep is my father's specialty, a trick that he perfected over years of similar situations. My mother decided to let him sleep, and by the time morning rolled around, the whole thing had completely slipped her mind. If my father's specialty is pretending to be asleep, my mother's is forgetting—particularly things that might make her realize her husband is not as good as she believes he is.

Several weeks later, my father picked me up from school with that woman in the car again. Was he going to make a habit of this? I sat in the stupid back seat with her annoying sons who were jumping back and forth over the seat.

Once again, we pulled up in front of her dilapidated house, but this time we all got out and went inside. The lady brought me a box of powdered donuts. I loved powdered donuts. "Maybe she isn't ugly after all," I thought to myself.

"Mommy, Daddy took me to the lady's house today, and she even gave me donuts," I said when I got home.

"Oh, she did."

"Yup."

She turned and walked into the bedroom where my father

had disappeared a few moments earlier, and I followed her. My father was stretched out on their queen-sized bed fully clothed, eyes closed.

This time my mom didn't even think about being polite. "Wake up," she hollered. "You better get up now. Where did you take my daughter this afternoon?"

Wearily he rolled over onto his back and began to rub the "sleep" from his eyes.

"Where did you take my daughter this afternoon?" she asked him again.

"Nowhere."

"Nowhere?" she asked in disbelief. "You sure you didn't stop off anywhere?"

"Yes. What is this all about?" my Daddy replied in his special I'm-tired-of-being-blamed-for-everything voice. "I can't even get any sleep in my own house."

"Then why did she tell me that she went to some lady's house?"

She swore she was getting a divorce, and, like a fool, I believed her.

Having that lady in the car must have been something really bad, I thought. I'd never seen my mother speak to my father like that.

"Oh, this friend at work asked me to help move his wife, so I went over there and helped pack a few boxes."

"That's all you did over there?"

"Yes."

"Then why did you tell me you went 'nowhere'?"

"Because I forgot," he said, as if warning her to drop the whole subject. "We didn't stay long."

"Oh, I'm sorry," she said, suddenly backing off. "I didn't mean to get so upset. I just don't like not knowing where you take her. She is my daughter."

"She's my daughter too," he said, suddenly on the offensive.

"I know that," she said meekly. "But I would at least like to be told."

That was the last time my daddy ever took me to that lady's house. From that day on, our relationship went downhill. He stopped confiding in me like he used to and I began to lose respect for him. I never told my mother that he kissed that woman, but I knew. My daddy who I believed could do no wrong had lied.

I never saw any women after that, but over the years, I heard about many. My father was never good at discretion. Friends of ours have spotted him all over the place—at clubs, parties, and strolling hand in hand on the street, and never with the same woman twice.

As the years went on, he was hardly ever around and we never did anything as a family. We didn't eat together, we didn't go out together. By the time I was in junior high school, we'd even stopped watching movies together on Friday nights—a sacred ritual.

My father never said more than two words to me and my sister: "Good morning" and "Good night." He treated us as if we no longer existed in his life.

As I got older, the way he treated my mother and the disrespect he showed for our family made me more and more angry. When my mother and I talked about it, I would tell her that it didn't matter to me, that I really didn't care. But I was lying to my mother and to myself.

"Why don't you just kick him out?" I asked my mother one day when I couldn't stand living in the same house with him anymore.

"Because I love him. When you get married, then you'll understand," she said.

But I don't think I ever will.

One day when I was in the 7th grade, I came home from school and found my mother home in the middle of the afternoon. She was sitting on the living room floor still dressed in her business suit, with her legs crossed and her head in her lap. I could hear the heart-wrenching sobs. My heart just broke. I felt helpless. I knew that whatever was wrong, it must be really bad. The only time I had ever seen my mother shed a tear was at my aunt's funeral.

She told me to go upstairs and do my homework. Then I heard the front door slam. I raced to the bathroom window, and saw my mom's car zoom out of the driveway. I started to panic. Where was she going in such a hurry? What if she got into an accident? Then what would I do? My life would be over.

I stayed awake all night waiting for my Mom to come back. She didn't get home until about 4:30 the next afternoon. She came walking into my room still dressed in yesterday's business suit, acting as if she had never been gone. She had a thick envelope in her hand.

"Look at this," she said, handing me a document printed on beige stationery with the name of a law firm at the top. Despite all the legal jargon, I understood what it said: my father had gotten one of his whores pregnant, and now he was being sued for child support.

When I had finished reading it, I handed it back to her.

"You don't have anything to say?" she asked.

"No," I said. "What did you expect? He ain't nothing but a ho, somebody had to get pregnant sometime."

"I know that," she said. "But now people might find out."

"Find out what?"

"That he's sleeping around."

"Oh please, Mommy."

So that's why she spent the entire day crying, because people might find out! People had already found out. Instead of worrying about her health (he could have brought home some nasty disease), or her marriage, she was worrying about preserving the image of our perfect family. She put the document back into the envelope and left. I had nothing left to say to her.

That night, my father came home early. I was both surprised and scared. As soon as he stepped through the door my mother started yelling at him. "You bastard! You bastard!" she screamed at the top of her lungs.

He just stood there looking confused. "What's wrong? What are you talking about?" My mother probably would have fallen for it again, but this time she had written proof.

She kept on yelling until he became angry. It was summertime and people were outside chilling on their front stoops. My father hates being embarrassed.

Suddenly, he hit her. He hit my mommy! I was watching from the top of the stairs where I had been all along. I heard the sound and saw her drop like a rag doll. I started to run downstairs. "Get back upstairs now," he ordered me.

"Leave me alone!" I yelled, trying to keep the fear out of my voice.

"I said get back upstairs now," he ordered once again. He stood there at the bottom of the steps, staring up at me with this hateful look on his face.

"Go to hell, you ho," I said.

As soon as the words came out of my mouth I regretted saying them. He came running up the stairs really fast, but I was faster. I ran into my room, slammed the door and locked it.

"Open this damned door!" he screamed and started trying to break it down with his fists.

He had never raised his voice to me like that before, so I knew that if he got into my room, he was going to hurt me. He must have been crazy; there was no way I was going to open that door. I wasn't going to give him the chance to do to me what he had done to my mother.

I dragged one of my chairs over and sat down in front of the door. That was where I spent the night. Although everything got quiet after a while, fear kept me on guard. I didn't want him to try to hurt me. He had never done it before, but that night he had done a lot of things he had never done before.

Early the next morning, I slowly opened my door and peeked out. There was my father lying on his back in the middle of the hallway, sleeping. I tiptoed around him and hurried downstairs. My mother was sitting at the dining table with her head resting on her folded arms. "Mommy," I said gently as I nudged her arm.

When she lifted up her head, I could see the entire left side of her face was swollen. It looked disgusting. As tears rolled down my face, I ran to the refrigerator. "I hate you, I hate you, I hate you," I kept repeating under my breath. I filled a plastic bag with some ice, and I gave it to my mother to hold against her face.

When I feel like I just can't cope I go to my friend's house and soak up the luxurious feeling of security and peace and quiet.

She and I spent that day making plans; it's funny that it took something like that to bring us closer together. For the first time, we actually spoke openly about what was happening to our family, and about how it made me feel. "I am going to have to divorce him soon. We can't live like this," my mother said.

She will never know how long I had waited for her to say those words.

"Not soon, Mommy. Now."

"OK. I'll go see a lawyer tomorrow, during my lunch break. You know what?"

"What?"

"I never thought his whoring around affected you. You never told me anything. If you would have, I probably would have done this sooner. I don't want you to be unhappy."

I was shocked by that. I never thought it really mattered to her how I felt about it one way or another.

We agreed that she had to go to the lawyer the very next day. She couldn't live with a husband who beat her, and I couldn't stand to see her beaten. With her swollen face to remind her of how brutal her beloved husband could be, she finally understood that he had to go. I could learn to live without a father. I had already lost my daddy, the man I respected and in whom I could confide, so losing my father wouldn't make much difference.

My father went about his business as if nothing had happened. He even had the nerve to ignore us, as if we had done something wrong.

The next day came and went without a visit to the lawyer, but my mother promised me that I wouldn't have to worry about him ever hitting her again. She swore she was getting a divorce, and, like a fool, I believed her.

Well, it's now seven years and 14 beatings later. He continues to sleep around, and she continues to yell and scream about it (as if that will change anything). He gets angry and hits her, then the next day everything is back to normal—except for her swollen face.

For a while, my mother used to try to make excuses for my father's violent behavior. "He doesn't beat me up badly," she'd say, or, "He doesn't hit me more than twice." But I've learned to just drown her out. I don't even help her take down the swelling anymore. If she wants to take the beating, then she can deal with the results on her own. I tell her what I think she should do, but she never listens.

Although my father has not moved out of the house, he no longer treats me like his daughter. It's as if whatever was left of the bond we had broke the first night he laid hands on my mother. He doesn't even speak to me.

He doesn't support me financially or any other way either. He doesn't remember my birthday, and when he found out I was graduating from high school, he refused to come. Of all that he has done, that hurt me the most. Despite everything, he was still my father. It was the most important day in my life, and I couldn't have my entire family there.

My mommy saved the day, though. She was there for me,

trying her best to make up for his absence. "Don't worry, one day he'll change," she told me. Even though I knew it was nothing but an empty promise, still I held onto it, and I still do. I want to turn back time, and enjoy my family the way we once were. We weren't perfect, but we were happy. I keep hoping, like my mother, that one day he'll be a husband and a father again.

Meanwhile, the only thing that has changed since that day back in the 7th grade is that I have taken on the job of referee. While they yell, argue, throw things, and basically try to kill each other, I use whatever means possible to try to stop it.

Sometimes I throw myself between them. I yell threats such as, "I'm getting out of this house and never coming back!" at the top of my lungs, hoping that my voice will bring them out of their rage, but that seldom works either. When nothing works, I lock myself in my room and cry until I fall asleep, or I leave the house.

I must be a very weak person, because I still let it get to me. I still cry and I still get depressed. At times I feel like I can't take it anymore and I decide to move out, but I never do.

There are times when I just can't cope and I have thoughts of suicide. Rather than hurt myself, though, I go to my friend's house and soak up the luxurious feeling of security and peace and quiet. I'll spend the entire day hanging out with her father, joking around, and talking about anything at all. He even calls me his adopted daughter (I wish I was). Maybe all I'm doing is running away, but it works just fine for me.

In spite of it all, I have been able to keep up the facade of a good life. I have graduated from high school and started college. I am on my way to accomplishing my goals. I can't let this situation hold me down. If I do, then I will never get out of this hellhole.

Every time the arguing and fighting starts I tell myself that one of these days I'm going to just up and leave. I really want to. I have spent too many nights crying myself to sleep because my walls are not soundproof and I can hear the sound a fist makes when it hits flesh. Each night when I lay my head down to sleep, I pray that I won't have to wake up to screams of "Help!" and fulfill my duty.

I want to leave but if I do, who will be there to try to stop the arguing before it escalates into something more? Who will protect my mommy? My mommy needs someone to protect her. I have a younger sister, but she sometimes acts as if she doesn't care what happens. I may be the one person who keeps him from beating my mother to a pulp. So I guess I'll have to stay. But if I do I'll have to endure so much. I don't know what I'll do.

The author was in college when she wrote this story.

John Gaston

Dear Pops:
Why'd You Hit Mom?

By Antwaun Garcia

Dear Pops,

Wassup, Daddy? This is your boy writing. Since for some reason we can't see each other, and you seem like you don't have time for me, this letter is for you. This time, if you read this, you're gonna see my point of view on my childhood, my mother, and, of course, on you. I want you to feel my anger, Daddy! I hope you're ready for the truth inside your son.

At one point in my life I was happy calling you my father. I never blamed you for doing your thang. At the time, we were living in Harlem, and I always respected the way you had with the ladies. Every block you had some girl knowing your name, or sliding you her number. I looked up to you as more than a father. I looked up to you like a best friend. We would be on the block where everyone knew me as Lil' Chic, and you would tell them I was your number one son. Remember that, Daddy?

Then, when you got addicted to crack, I saw the transformation. I saw the way you treated Moms. You disrespected Moms like she was a ho in the street. Whenever something didn't go your way, Moms was your punching bag. Remember, Daddy?

Those times you beat Moms, I felt so helpless. All I could do was watch your anger heading towards Moms' body, with left slaps, left hooks, right slaps, and right hooks. I couldn't do nothing but hear Moms cry out, and no one was there to help her, at least not until I started to take the beatings. Remember that, Daddy?

I felt so helpless. All I could do was watch your anger heading towards Moms' body

That first time I fought back you finally realized you weren't fighting her anymore. You were fighting your second oldest son. I bet you never expected me to stand my ground and fight you man to boy, fist to fist, your hatred to my not understanding. I always loved you, but never loved the way you treated Moms.

Moms never wasted time calling the police on you, as you spent most of your time in and out of jail anyway. Every time I saw 5-0 arrest you, tears ran down my face. Uncle Mike would have to bring me in the house, because I was always ready to fight the cops for you. I thought that could help you go free. Remember that, Daddy?

Then you decided to take me out of Harlem, and let me spend time with you and Angie in the Bronx. What happened, Pops? I spent days watching you beating Angie, just like you did Moms. Remember that, Daddy?

From a newborn until the age of 9, I lived in poverty with Moms. Wasn't it your job to take care of business and get us out? Did you do that? Nah. We spent nights in the cold with no heat, summers with no AC. Rats and roaches ran in and out the crib like they had keys. I never had new clothes, no food, no water, no electricity. All this you put me through, yet I still hold love for you, love for all those times we spent together, the times we acted stupid, the times we had those conversations about the streets, life, struggles. Those are the times I hold dear.

Why do I still hold this love for you? I don't know why. I hold so much anger for you, yet underneath my hatred, I still hold so much love that has never been touched or revealed. The way you're going, it never will be.

How can you let me leave your life? How can you leave your so-called number one son? I was left with no choice but to move to Queens to live with relatives. Where were you when I had to leave Moms, Dad? Did you bother coming to get Shante and me and make us your family? No, Dad! Did you bother to come out to visit me? No. Right, Daddy? All those holidays, those birthdays, where were you? I only received cards from you in prison saying how much you wanted to be there, and that you could see me being happy with some candles on a cake in front of me.

I hold so much anger for you, yet underneath my hatred I still hold so much love.

All those times I spent mad at myself because I never saw you, never heard your voice. I thought it was somehow my doing. Soon four years had passed since I'd heard one word from you. Then you popped out of nowhere to make a visit.

I hung back, watching you get off the bus, you looking lost. Standing behind you next to the check cashing place, I kept my silence to see if you would notice your own child.

You saw me. You gave me a hug. For some reason, I couldn't move my arms to go round your body. Yours were aggressively pressed against me. When you let go, I stared dead in your eyes and you got your first view of my coldness. But your eyes were filled with relief and happiness.

I brought you to the house so you could finally see my sister, your fatherless daughter. She was nothing but happy seeing you. I could tell that by the way she came to you and hugged you so tight.

You see what you're doing to us, Dad? You see what kind of effect you have on us? And what do you do with that? You take advantage of us, like you did everything else in life.

The only joy I had from seeing you again was watching the way Shante and you were getting along, and how happy it made her to be with you. Seeing the way you two played reminded me of the way we used to, and how happy it made me. Remember those days, wrestling on the bed, playing basketball in the streets? Those are the days I miss most, the days when I was your son and you my father.

Now I can't help the way I'm feeling. You put all this hatred in me. You gave me all these unloved feelings I hold so deep. Why, Dad? Why'd you do it? What did Moms ever do to you? What did I ever do to you? I only asked you to be a father to me, and be the best father you could be. Since you can't do your part, I can't fulfill my part, either. I can't be your son.

But I still miss you, Pops.

Antwaun was 18 when he wrote this story.

Turning Her In

By Anonymous

I always worried that I'd be considered a snitch for telling on my sister. My brother told me that I had messed everything up. But I had finally decided that I'd had enough.

When my sister got custody of my brother and me two years ago, everything was good in the beginning. Fatima, who'd always been a mother figure to me, had been trying to get custody of us for about 10 years, since she turned 18. She always told us that she wanted all of us to be together.

When I was 8, my brother and I went to live with my aunt in New Jersey. My sister would come to visit us during the holidays and summers, and she always brought me gifts on Christmas and my birthday.

Her visits were a much-needed break from my aunt, who was verbally and physically abusive. During the difficult times,

Fatima (next to my brother) was my main source of comfort. But before she could get things together to get custody of us, the agency found out about the abuse in my aunt's household and my brother and I were sent to a foster home in Brooklyn.

A year later, Fatima finally got custody of us. But by then I had mixed feelings about it because my mother (who is addicted to crack) and Fatima's boyfriend, Haze, would be living with us in a one-and-a-half-bedroom apartment, and Fatima was expecting a baby. Fatima kept telling me that she was going to find a bigger space for us, just give her time.

When I first moved in with my sister, I thought that living with my mom would be a big challenge. It only took a few days for me to realize we had a much bigger problem: Haze.

From the day I first met him I didn't like him. He was an aspiring rapper, very cocky, wore the baggy clothes and smoked. I noticed he was disrespectful to Fatima. He'd cut her off and tell her to shut up. Of course she'd pick a fight with him afterward to show us she could stand up for herself. But I soon realized that was all just talk.

Whatever Haze wanted, she would get it for him. I'd seen her stand up to her previous boyfriends, and I had no idea who this new Fatima was.

The first time I saw things get physical was two days before my sister's baby shower. My brother and Haze came upstairs punching one another. My brother cursed at Haze and said, "You're not my father."

"I'm not, but you gonna respect me," Haze said. He threw my brother on the floor, putting him in a headlock and choking him. I thought Haze was going to kill him.

My sister came out to break it up and Haze pushed her. I didn't like that at all, so I grabbed a knife from the kitchen.

"Yo, don't be pushing my sister, she's pregnant. And let my brother go!"

I didn't actually think I was going to stab anyone, but I felt like I could if I had to. My sister tried to loosen the grip of Haze's hands from around my brother's neck.

"Let him go…let him go…he has asthma!"

Haze finally let my brother go. "You lucky, son. She just saved your life."

My brother and I tried to leave, but my sister locked the front door.

"Y'all not going nowhere, it's 12 at night," she said, blocking the way for us to get out.

"Come on now, Fatima, you're always sticking up for him, always," my brother said. "You don't even care 'bout us!"

I guess I blocked out what happened after that. The next thing I remember, my sister was choking me, telling me that she hated me and wished that I were dead. At that point I really didn't care about what happened to Fatima. I never imagined in a million years that my sister, my protector, would be choking me.

Whatever Haze wanted, she would get it for him. I had no idea who this new Fatima was.

I really thought she was going to kill me. I hated her for putting her hands on me. I felt betrayed. She was getting mad at me and my brother instead of her boyfriend. I hadn't done anything but try to help her.

After that my brother and I talked about reporting Fatima to children's services, but I wasn't ready. Fatima kept telling me that things were going to get better and that we'd be moving to Jersey. By moving to Jersey, I thought she meant getting away from Haze. I convinced myself that Fatima would return to her old self and we'd be OK again once he was out of the picture.

Meanwhile, the fighting continued. My brother and I tried to help, but she always told us to "stay in a child's place." So we just listened to her cries for help from the other side of the wall. Sometimes we even laughed at her stupidity, but I knew deep down inside it hurt us both to hear this and not do anything about it.

Last January, Fatima finally moved us to a bigger house in New Jersey. But it was a bittersweet start. Haze was still living with us, and he and Fatima were up to the same tricks, even after their baby boy was born.

After a couple of weeks, though, they broke up. Fatima kicked Haze out and he moved back to New York. But he still came around, and the violence continued.

By mid-June my sister was spending a lot of time in New York. Meanwhile my brother and I were stuck in the house with no cable or phone cause my sister wasn't paying the bills.

One morning my sister came back home and told us to pack our things because we were going to New York for the weekend. That weekend ended up being weeks, and weeks became months.

Eventually, my brother went back to Jersey to stay with my aunt because he'd found a job there. My sister was staying with Haze in Manhattan. I was staying with my cousins in the Bronx. We later found out we'd been kicked out of the house in Jersey because Fatima hadn't paid the rent for months.

One day, my cousin, also a rapper, was making beats in his studio and called me in to ask for my opinion.

"That's hot, you gonna let me get on a track?" I asked.

"How about this, you write something up and I'll do the same," he told me.

Five minutes later I came back in the room with my verse written up. It was all about what I'd been going through with Fatima. I told my cousin I didn't want to read it out loud, but he insisted. I cleared my throat and started:

"We been evicted before, so your hard knocks mean nothing to me/I don't tell my life story because I don't feed on sympathy/I gotta feed myself, cause ain't no one feeding me."

After I'd finished the whole verse, he was speechless. His mouth dropped, and he called his wife over.

"Kali, Kali, read this," he said, handing her the sheet of paper.

Once she read it she looked at me with the same expression as her husband.

"Is this true?" she asked me.

"Yeah."

"When did this happen?"

"Now."

"Wait, this is happening right now? That's why Fatima told you to stay here?"

I shrugged my shoulders. "I guess."

At the time, I didn't realize that this was my way of asking for help. The whole night they tried to convince me to tell child welfare about my sister abusing me and about our living situation. I didn't know what to do. I decided to wait until after I returned from a week-long camp, where I had been going for the past two summers.

I was a little quiet at camp and my camp social worker began asking me questions about "how everything was at home." Pressure had been building up inside of me and I cracked. I'd known her for a couple of years so I trusted her, and the whole story came pouring out.

The next day she sat me down. She wanted me to tell ACS (the local child welfare agency) immediately. I still wasn't sure, but I just wanted to get it off my chest. Afterwards I called my brother and told him that I had told ACS everything.

"What you do that for? Man, you just messed everything up," he said.

"They gonna find out anyway, dummy," I said.

"Man, you a snitch," he said, then hung up.

I found out that after hanging up with me he had called my sister and told her what I'd done. I felt betrayed. To make matters worse, our agency reacted to my report with shock and suspicion, as if I'd made the story up. They called my brother and he denied everything, so they looked at me as a liar.

I was disgusted with the agency. They were the ones who

hadn't been doing their job. If they'd been keeping better track of where we were and what was going on in the house, I wouldn't have been put in the position of having to report my own sister.

I understood why my brother didn't want Fatima to be reported. He wanted to stay in Jersey to finish up school so he could graduate on time and keep his job. Me "snitching" messed up his chances for all that. He was getting his life together and I respected that.

But what about me? I wasn't working and I had no money. I also wasn't in Jersey where I would be able to graduate on time like him. So why shouldn't I make a better life for myself, too? I didn't want to worry about where I would be living next or whether my sister would be there when I woke up.

As soon as camp was over ACS moved my brother and me back with our old foster family in Brooklyn. A couple of days later, my foster mother told me she had spoken to my brother and he said he wasn't mad at me anymore. She said he understood where I was coming from. But my brother and I never talked about it again. I think we both just wanted to move on.

I convinced myself that Fatima would return to her old self and we'd be OK again once he was out of the picture.

The first weeks back with my foster family I went into a depression. I wasn't eating or talking much. Sometimes I just felt numb, and I would lie in the dark all the time. I was exhausted, trying to make sense of everything. I felt like I was moving backwards, adjusting all over again to the foster family I'd been living with a year ago.

But with time, I did adjust. I had to. I had nowhere else to go. My foster mother really helped me through things by reaching out to me. She'd make me get up when I just wanted to lie in bed. Her encouragement reminded me that life still goes on.

It's been nine months now, and my brother and I are doing great. Our guardian actually listens to us, we receive our weekly spending money, and there's no abuse.

The whole situation with my sister has taught me to start looking out for me, and that's something I'll remember in future relationships. I can't stop her from dating Haze, but I won't spend time with her if he's involved. That's one thing I'm not willing to compromise.

All of her verbal and physical abuse is something I'm not going to forget. I don't know if I'll ever be able to build a good relationship with my sister. But in the end I know I did the right thing by speaking up.

My whole life I was brought up to believe snitching is wrong, and I worried about the consequences of reporting my sister. But till this day I don't look at myself as a snitch.

When you're snitching, you're telling on someone else. When you speak out, you're standing up for yourself and others with cause. I stood up for myself and my brother. The outcome of that was losing a friendship with my sister, but gaining respect and control over my life.

The author was in high school when she wrote this story.

Gamal Jones

'It's Not Your Fault'
How to deal when there's violence at home

Heather McLain, a domestic violence expert, answers our questions.

Q: If your parent is in a violent relationship, what can you do about it?

A: First of all, young people need to know that they are not to blame for a parent's situation. Domestic violence is never the fault of children or teens.

If your parent is in a violent or abusive relationship it's important for you to keep yourself safe. That means staying out of the room if a fight is happening instead of getting into the middle of it to protect your parent. You should avoid rooms where you can be trapped or where there are weapons. You can go to a neighbor's house to get help or even call the police. The last thing a parent who is being abused wants is for their child to be injured.

It may be possible to talk with your parent about the abuse

when the abuser is not around, and share how you feel about the violence. But remember that violent relationships are very complicated. You can't expect that the relationship will end just because of this conversation.

Finally, you can find someone outside the family to talk with about the abuse going on at home. You can always call the national 24-hour domestic violence hotline 1-800-799-SAFE (7233) and talk to someone anonymously. The people who answer the hotline are trained in dealing with violent relationships and can help young people and adults figure out what they can do and how to stay safe.

Q: If you tell someone that domestic violence is going on in your home, will they put you in foster care?

A: ACS, the child welfare system in New York, has guidelines about what to do when a parent is in a violent relationship. Different states have slightly different rules, but in New York workers need to make what are called "reasonable efforts" to help the parent and youth get what they need to stay safe and to stay together. This can include helping the parent get an order of protection to keep the abuser away from the family, helping the parent move to a domestic violence shelter in order to be safe, and/or connecting the parent, the young person, and even the abuser to services that can help them all address and recover from the abuse.

It is not your responsibility to help your parent recover.

If the violence is so severe that it poses an immediate danger to the life or health of the young person, ACS may have to place the youth in foster care. But cases that dangerous are fairly rare.

Q: How does witnessing domestic violence affect children and teens?

A: Every young person is affected in a different way when they witness domestic violence. You should know that whatever you're feeling is normal.

Some common things that young people experience are feelings of sadness, not wanting to go to school, not wanting to be away from your parent, feeling like you can't sleep or that you want to sleep all the time, having memories of the violence pop into your head at any time, feeling angry, getting into fights or not wanting to hang out with friends. Sometimes young people feel so badly about the violence that they want to hurt or kill themselves.

Q: How can you recover from living in a violent home?

A: Again, the first thing to remember is that the violence is not your fault and that you are not alone. Many people have been through this and there are a lot of people who can help.

Call the domestic violence hotline or talk to an adult you trust. It's important not to keep your feelings inside because over time those feelings can make you feel depressed or angry. You deserve to get the support you need so that you aren't affected by the violence forever.

Q: How can you help your parent recover?

A: It is not your responsibility to help your parent recover, but you can offer them love and support. This doesn't mean that you have to pretend that you don't have your own feelings about the abuse. What's important is to have the chance to share your feelings about what happened.

You may love or feel angry with both parents, or you may side with one against the other. It can be really difficult to have those feelings. The best thing to do is to find a safe adult to speak to.

---

*Heather McLain, MSW, was the Community Coordinator
for Domestic Violence Policy and Planning at ACS,
New York City's child welfare agency.*

Part II: Dating Violence

Breaking Free

By Anonymous

I met Lucas one November night at the movie theater in our neighborhood. I asked him for a match to light my cigarette. He asked if I had a man and I told him no. I didn't think he was cute at first, but he had a boyish look that caught my attention. We exchanged phone numbers and the next day he called me.

We spent the whole day together. We went to my house and I introduced him to my mom, who thought he was very sweet. Later on, he asked me to be his girlfriend and I said yes. From that day on we were inseparable. The only time we were apart was during school.

Our relationship moved quickly. After being together for one month we had sex for the first time and I got pregnant. I wanted to have an abortion but obstacles got in my way until it was too late. So I ended up keeping the baby.

During the last four months of my pregnancy I was placed in a maternity shelter. Lucas's mother filed for my guardianship so I wouldn't have to stay in foster care. When our baby was six weeks old, we moved into Lucas's mother's house. Lucas and I were excited about living together, but neither of us knew what the future had in store.

The first month was fun. Lucas helped me move my things in and we began to plan. We talked about getting married, finding an apartment, saving money, and so on. We were happy with the new family we had created.

We both had dated other people in the past, but this was the longest either one of us had been in a relationship. It was nice to be in love and have our beautiful little boy. It made me feel older, like I had settled my life down instead of being a crazy teenager.

Then I began to see a side of Lucas that I had never seen before. He started telling me what to wear, how to do my hair, and when to wear make-up. Then he started making me clean his room, cook, wash dishes, and do laundry for him. He was treating me as if I were his property instead of his girlfriend.

I thought doing things your man wanted was what love was about.

At first he would just ask me to do things or wear certain things and I would do him favors because I cared for him so much. I thought doing things your man wanted was what love was about. But after a while, he became more demanding.

Sometimes I refused to do what he wanted me to do, and he would get violent. So I tried to avoid his temper. If I had homework, it had to wait until I finished the chores he gave me, even if that meant doing it on the train the next morning.

Then Lucas started going out and drinking. When he came home drunk, he'd call me a whore, a b-tch, and any other name he could think of to hurt me. Sometimes he would come home when I was asleep and just start hitting me. I would wake up crying, and he'd tell me to shut up because it was me that caused him to act that way.

When I started disobeying Lucas's orders and trying to stand up for myself, he would hit me. If he didn't like the outfit I chose to wear to school, he'd tell me to change. If I didn't, he'd tell me I wasn't going to school. I'd try to leave and he'd follow me into the hall and slap or choke me and call me a slut.

I sometimes felt like a little girl trying to sneak around and do the things her parents said she couldn't. When I got caught, I got a beating. I knew things were out of hand.

I didn't grow up in a traditional home with a wife and husband, but I had heard about the old-fashioned way of living where it is the woman's place to take care of the housework and the children while the man goes to work. For a while I decided that Lucas was just playing the role of how a husband is supposed to be. I thought I was supposed to do the housework in order to take the position of a wife and mother.

Later, when I realized that no husband should treat his wife the way Lucas treated me, I made up more ridiculous excuses for his behavior. I'd think, "It's my own fault. If I just did as he asked I could have avoided it," or, "Maybe he's right and I just don't realize it yet."

When I remembered that Lucas was the only guy I'd been with who had acted this way with me, I would tell myself that every relationship is different so I really couldn't compare Lucas to my exes.

Other times I'd feel sorry for Lucas. After all, his mother was extremely abusive. She had foster kids she abused. She hit them with a belt, hit them in the mouth until they bled, and gave them ice cold baths. She seemed to always have to be in control of something. Lucas had told me that she had also abused him. So I told myself that Lucas couldn't help his controlling and abusive ways. That's what he grew up with.

Now I feel bit ashamed that I could have been so stupid as to force myself to believe that I was the one to blame, or that Lucas wasn't responsible for how he treated me. I think I really wanted to hold onto Lucas for my son, and I knew that if I left him I'd have to go into foster care. For some reason I also still loved Lucas. Every time he said something nice or we had a romantic moment, hope of him changing his ways flooded my heart.

I think I realized things were out of hand when I thought about my relationship with my mom. She and I didn't get along very well and I never did anything she told me to. So why was I listening to Lucas? He was about the same age as me, definitely nowhere near as smart as me, and he thought he could control my life. I wasn't about to let him take me over and pull me down. Unfortunately, it was already happening. My realization made me want to get away, but I was still afraid of what he would do to me if I left or where I would end up.

Every time he said something nice or we had a romantic moment, hope of him changing his ways flooded my heart.

So I tried to get away by meeting a new guy at my school. Joey and I started talking and hanging out together in school and sometimes I managed to talk to him on the phone when Lucas was out drinking. I told Joey what was going on with Lucas and it upset him. It was a relief to find someone to tell my whole situation to without being criticized. I liked Joey a lot.

All of my friends and my cheerleading coaches noticed that I was like a different person during the time that I was seeing Joey. I was so much happier because I found someone who appreciated and respected me. I was still living with Lucas, though, and the time came when he found out about Joey. He wanted me to tell him where Joey lived. He wanted to fight him.

When I refused, he punched me in the face and busted my lip. He said that if I didn't let him fight Joey he would make me take the hits instead. Lucas ended up finding out Joey's phone number, calling him, and threatening that if he even spoke to me he would beat him up. Joey didn't want to be involved in any trouble, so he decided that we should separate.

After a while everything calmed down but I was right back to where I was before I met Joey, still dealing with the abuse.

Finally, I started talking about it. At school, a cheerleading competition was coming up and Lucas was threatening to not let me go. So I went to my coach to explain. I was afraid, but I decided to tell her the truth. I knew that if I didn't, I might be kicked off the team. There was no way anyone was going to make me give up cheerleading, something I had put the last six years of my life into. I let that determination push me to tell my coach what was going on.

As I talked to her, the truth came out about what was really going on with Lucas and me. I let her know that Lucas was abusing me and that was why I'd been missing classes and not handing in my homework.

My coach tried to convince me to get help. But when I thought about leaving Lucas, I was afraid of how he might react. I was also afraid of going back into foster care and losing my son. So even though I knew what was happening was wrong, I kept dealing with him and hoping for the best.

Then one night after Lucas hit me, I went to a friend's house and told her what was going on. She advised me to go to my social worker with the truth. The next morning, I did. My social worker gave me permission to stay at my mom's house for the weekend.

On Sunday, Lucas and his mother came to my mom's with a missing person report. Lucas' mother told the police that I ran away and abandoned my son. The police told her that if I didn't come home my baby could be taken away from me. I felt furious that the police didn't care that I was being abused. To avoid losing my son, I returned to the hellhole that I had to call home.

As soon as we got there, the abuse began again. But my social worker had listened to me, and soon she moved me out of Lucas's house and into a foster home. Then Lucas began to treat me better than he ever did. I still loved him, and I convinced myself that it was the pressures of living together that had made him act the way he did. I wanted things to work out so that my son could have a father. So Lucas and I started seeing each other again.

There were good times between us—sweet words exchanged, kind gestures—and Lucas had 101 apologies for the way he had been treating me. They made me feel that there was hope of things working out between us.

But it only took a few weeks for him to start all over again. This time it wasn't as bad because I was able to go home to my foster home in Brooklyn every night, far away from him. His abuse kept on throughout the summer and by October, almost two years after we'd first met, we were broken up again.

On our two-year anniversary I received a letter from Lucas saying "Happy Anniversary." It made me cry. Despite everything, I still loved him. I still don't understand why. Maybe just because we'd been through so much together. It upset me that I could love him so much and still have things be so bad.

Just over two years ago, I had never met Lucas. I had never been in foster care. I was a virgin. I had never been beaten by a boyfriend. Now all that's changed.

I wondered if Lucas was the best man I'd ever had. I worried that I wouldn't feel the same about anyone else. I didn't want to admit that the father of my son and I couldn't work things out. So I called him. He told me that he was willing to change. He seemed sincere. I decided to give him another chance.

For a short time, everything felt different. Lucas bought me things. He let me do whatever I wanted. He didn't dare raise a hand to me. I was so happy. I had back the boyfriend I had when we first got together.

But then I saw his old ways coming back, and I broke up with him. We didn't speak for another month, and then Lucas came to my school threatening me. That day he followed me home and threatened my family, my friends, and me. I got an order of protection against him. One night, he broke our kitchen window. My aunt called the police. Lucas was arrested. He was put in jail and I followed through with trying to keep him there.

Before I met Lucas I called women stupid if they stayed in abusive relationships. I'm shocked that it happened to me, because I didn't think it ever would. But then again, who does?

Right now Lucas is out of jail and he has been calling my home and my mother's house asking all kinds of questions about where I am. No one gives him any information. At this point, there is no way I am ever getting back with him. There are too many people among my family and friends who love me too much for me to waste my time and energy on a guy who abuses me.

I also realize that my son deserves a better life than to see his mother get beaten up all the time. The way things were going, he may not have had a mother for long.

In future relationships, I hope to be much more careful about noticing early signs of abuse. It seems that if you allow abuse to happen once you can lose control for a long time before you get your life back in order.

It's weird how meeting one person can change your life so much. Just over two years ago, I had never met Lucas. I had never been in foster care. I was a virgin. I had never been beaten by a boyfriend. Now all that's changed, and I can't take any of it back. It will probably follow me in one form or another for a long time, maybe forever.

The writer was in high school when she wrote this story.

Handel Morency

Putting Up With Her Hands

By Derrick B.

I'm 18, weigh 178 lbs and stand 5'11". I don't like to show emotion but always try to keep a smile on my face. Looking at me, you'd never know that my girlfriend uses me as a punching bag.

I got used to getting hit by women when I was young. I felt that my grandmother hit me out of love and my mother hit me out of hate, but with my current girlfriend, Linda (not her real name), I don't know what to think. Does she hit me because she loves me and is frustrated that I don't understand her? Does she hit me because she has an anger problem? I'm not sure of the reason, but one thing I do know: I'm afraid of what might happen.

My grandmother raised me until I was 7. She was a Christian, took me to church on Sundays and tried to raise me as a gentleman. She did not believe in hitting or spanking me unless she felt I needed to learn an important lesson.

One time, when I was about to enter a store before her, she gave me a quick slap up side my head.

"Ouch!" I yelled, confused.

"Didn't I teach you any manners? Ladies first," said my grandmother. She smiled and rubbed the spot where she hit me. Her smiling and rubbing me made me think that she hit me out of love. This seemed okay to me because she was trying to make me a better person and raise me well.

When I met my mom a couple weeks after my 7th birthday, I fell in love at first sight.

After my mom was released from a center where she was treated for abusing drugs and drinking, I moved in with her. But by the time I turned 8, she had gone back to her old habits. My mom gave birth to my baby brother when I was 9, and I had to take care of him. When my mother left us alone to get drugs, I struggled to clean and cook, care for my newborn brother, and do homework without any help.

I wished my mother would love me the way I loved her, but no matter what I did she never showed me affection. Instead, she beat me for no reason with bats, brooms, and anything else she could grab. If I was late doing a chore, she'd scream, "When I tell you to do something, you do it!" She called me "stupid" and cursed me for being born. If she blamed me for something I didn't deserve, she would swear she was right. Her beatings didn't feel the same as my grandmother's. Her beatings felt like they came from hate.

I started to feel like I had a split personality: One part of me wanted to yell and curse back at my mother. But the other half won. That was the half that chose to live with the abuse, stay quiet, and keep the love I had for her.

When I got older, I began to think my mom took advantage of me because I was born with a soft heart, so I decided to prove I was hard. By age 14, I was a troublemaker: stealing from stores, throwing things at girls to make them mad, and hanging with "bad" kids who gave me the attention that I never got from my mom.

One day, my mother took me to a big building in Manhattan and told me to have a seat. I heard her tell the lady at the front desk that she was through with me and wanted to put me in "placement." The lady told her she would have to go to court before that could happen. My mom said she was going out to smoke a quick cigarette. She never came back.

I thought, "My mom must really hate me."

I moved from group home to group home, causing trouble everywhere I went—robbing people, stealing from stores, and using girls for sex. I lost my feelings for the world and everybody in it.

Staying on a positive path for myself, without love, seems so meaningless and boring.

I lied to lots of girls and broke their hearts. I was angry over the way my mother rejected me and wanted other females to feel the same way. At first I enjoyed seeing them cry over me. No matter how many times I lied to them or used them, they always came back. I understood why. If my moms asked me back, I would have gone.

One night, I got in trouble with a friend and had to spend the night and part of the next day in the "bounds" room of the group home, a locked isolation chamber where you're supposed to think about what you did wrong.

Alone with my thoughts, I started having flashbacks of my life. I thought about all the innocent people I robbed when I could have gotten a job. I thought about all the females I used to satisfy my sexual desires. Tears rolled down my face.

It seemed as if God was asking me, "Do you want to live alone forever, taking your anger out on people who love you? Why do you treat people wrong because you were treated wrong? Is that the kind of person you really are?" To this day, I'm not sure who was talking—whether the voice was God's, or just something inside of me.

At that moment, my friend pointed out a female on the other side of the window. She was beautiful, with long black hair, brown eyes, a perfect smile, and a body like "Oh my god!" She looked like an angel.

After staff unlocked the door and told us we were free, I met this "angel." Her name was Linda and she was the roommate of a friend of mine.

It became clear right away that we would be together. Because she was the first person I'd seen when I was thinking about making big changes in my life, I felt Linda was special and different from all other girls. She also wanted me to change to be better. I thought she was an angel sent by God to help me.

During our first day together, she asked me, "Why do you wear that do-rag?"

"I like the way it makes me look," I answered.

"I don't," she said, and grabbed it off my head. She was smiling, and put it in her back pocket. I reached for it, but right at that moment she caught me off guard and kissed me. Instead of fighting back all my warm feelings for her, I accepted them. I didn't want to hurt her, but to love her.

I stopped seeing all the girls I played and spent most of my time going to movies and shopping with Linda. I opened up to her and told her all my dreams and secrets that I never told anyone else.

I felt gentle and calm with her. Whenever I did something positive, Linda would tell me how good I was and my ego would fly. She made me feel so special I hardly even thought about negative things. I called her every night just to talk.

I decided that I should quit drinking and drugging so I could spend my life with such a caring and understanding person. I realized I really loved this girl and that the negative things I was doing made her upset. I took my lighter and cigarettes and threw them in the trash.

It took me a while to change, but I did. My grades went from a 65 average to a 98. I stopped drinking and smoking cigarettes. To keep my mind off weed, I started boxing at the YMCA. When my friends asked me to come chill with them and smoke, I'd think about what Linda had said: "Derrick, you don't need your friends to prove to you that you're a king. I love you and I will always be around to support your dreams." Remembering her words, I thought about how good it felt to be loved. That gave me the confidence to say no.

However, as time passed I encountered a new problem—Linda and her hands. Two months after we got together, I said something Linda didn't like and she smacked me in the mouth.

My lip started bleeding.

"I'm sorry! That was an accident," said Linda. I forgave her right away.

A couple of months after that, Linda and I were filling out job applications. I spotted a digital camera I liked in a Radio Shack and went to look at it.

Every day I feel like I should leave. But Linda always says she's sorry and I always forgive her.

"Wow! Look at this camera!" I said. I was so excited I wanted to buy it right on the spot.

"Derrick, come on," said Linda. I ignored her and kept looking at the other products.

"Derrick! Come on so we can get on the bus!" yelled Linda.

"Wait! You act like we ain't got all day!" I said. Then she punched me in the eye.

I blacked out for a second. Then I felt like tearing her neck off. I saw her as my mother and all the anger I had inside came rushing back. I marched out of the store.

Linda chased me out of the store, screaming that she was sorry. I turned around wanting to beat the hell out of her. Instead, I threw a bus pass at her and said, "Since you want to act stupid so bad, get on the bus without me." Then I hopped in a cab, went back to the campus and smoked off all my stress with a friend.

Since then, Linda has hit me fairly regularly. There are several situations that can lead to it. If Linda is angry or thinks I'm ignoring her, I'm likely to get hit. Jealousy causes problems, too. She thinks I'm talking to other girls on the Internet. (I do, but I'm only getting advice from them to make my relationship with her better.)

She always makes me feel that the violence is all my fault. My mom did that, too. If I ask Linda about something wrong she did to me, she just says, "Why are you in placement?"

The situation is so confusing and stressful. I worry that one day when Linda hits me I'll let out all my anger. I might lose control, hit her back and end up in jail. I never want that to happen.

Every day I feel like I should break up with her. I'm tired of looking stupid, feeling stupid, and being called stupid. I'm also tired of getting my feelings hurt. But Linda always says she's sorry and I always forgive her. One nice "hi" and I forget her being mean. This makes me think: What if she could change?

To be honest, I think the violence is both our faults. Linda is in anger management classes, but she doesn't go. She feels she can handle her own problems. I don't think that's true. She needs to learn how to control her hands.

But I put up with her hands. I give both my mom and Linda the power to behave badly towards me. I wonder if women feel free to talk and act any way they want with me because I'm so quiet and rarely express my thoughts and opinions. Maybe I don't think I deserve to be in a non-hitting relationship because I've never had one. It would be weird to not feel something I've felt my whole life.

My grandmother taught me to walk away from trouble, but I can't walk away from Linda. I got no attention and acknowledgment as a child and now that I have some, I don't want to lose it.

I'm also afraid of what might happen if I do. I depend on her compliments. The kisses and smiles she gives me every time I do something good make me light on my feet. If I break up with her,

I will feel I wasted all of my time changing for nothing. I'll turn back to my old outlaw ways because staying on a positive path for myself, without love, seems so meaningless and boring.

Also, I feel compassion for Linda. How can I walk away from someone who has done me so much good? I really believe that one day she will change and stop hitting me and we can have a peaceful and healthy relationship.

I feel God must have brought us together for a reason. Still, I wonder, "Is this how love is supposed to feel?"

Derrick was 18 when he wrote this story.

Paulina Korkuz

If You Love Me, Don't Hit Me

By Latonya Williams

My friend Jessica has been going out with a guy named Kenyatta for three years. They are in love and she thinks he is the flyest guy out there. Every time I speak to her she's always saying, "Oh Tonya, look what Kenyatta brought me. Ain't this fly?"

Kenyatta treated her like a queen in the beginning of their relationship, buying her gifts and saying sweet things to her. I remember one time we were walking past a shoe store and Jessica said, "Yo, Tonya, those are the Tims my baby gonna get me for Christmas."

For a long time I thought they were a perfect couple and I wanted a man just like Kenyatta. Who wouldn't want a man who kept his girl looking fly all the time and treated her like she was royalty?

Jessica could talk to Kenyatta about anything, even female

matters, and he always understood. Not to mention the fact that Kenyatta's a dime-piece and all the girls wanted him. Things seemed to be perfect and I was mad happy for her.

At least that's what I thought, until one day last year, when Jessica came downstairs with a black eye. When she told me Kenyatta did it, I almost cried.

She tried to take up for him by saying, "Nah, girl, it ain't nothing, he found out about that guy we met, and you know, he got a temper. I'd rather have my boo care about me enough to hit me than not to give a damn at all."

Two weeks earlier, Jessica and I had been on our way to the store and this guy had tried to talk to her. They exchanged numbers, but she told him she had a man so they ended up just being friends. Obviously, Kenyatta didn't see it like that.

I always thought Jessica had the sense to know that when your man gives you a black eye, it's time to pick up and go.

When she tried to make excuses for Kenyatta's actions, I just looked at her and shook my head. I always thought Jessica had the sense to know that when your man gives you a black eye, it's time to pick up and go.

The black eye incident happened about a year ago and Jessica is still with him. Jessica and I ain't all that cool now, because she moved and we grew farther apart. Now I only see her once in a while when she comes out to Brooklyn to visit her grandmother and to see Kenyatta.

While we were still cool I used to speak to Jessica a lot about Kenyatta smacking her. I had only seen him hit her once, but she would tell me how he hit her on other occasions. I would tell her she should leave him because something must be wrong if he's hitting on her. The response I always seemed to get was, "I know, but Tonya you don't understand, that's my baby, I love him. He always says sorry when he hits me, and he be crying with me."

I can't imagine loving a guy who beats on me. When you

have a man, your appearance and your spirit are supposed to be good. If your man is abusing you, you're gonna look toe up and you're gonna feel toe up (toe up means messed up), so that is not good for you.

J essica is not the only teen I know in an abusive relationship. I know other girls who put up with guys who abuse them. Not all of them are getting hit. Some girls I know are in relationships with guys who abuse them emotionally. These girls always seem to think their boyfriend is the best they can get. I don't know what it is that makes these girls love their boyfriends so much, all I know is they will do anything for them.

For example, my homegirl Beverly, who's 17, is in a relationship with a 33-year-old man named Cortlandt. At first he seemed wonderful, a dime-piece, the whole nine. He would take Beverly anywhere she wanted to go and buy her anything she wanted. But no matter what Beverly wants to do, she can't do it if it doesn't involve him. She has to ask his permission to go to school because he thinks she should be home keeping him company.

Before she met him, Bev used to have a 4.0 average. She always kept her hair done and she and her grandmother had the best relationship. Now she lets herself go and neglects her school work. Cortlandt makes her feel like she's nothing when she leaves him. His demands have started problems between Bev and her family.

Beverly told me she stays with Cortlandt because she thinks that no one is gonna love her like he does.

I think Jessica and Bev are whipped. They're addicted to the affection that their man is giving them. They believe their man is God's gift, and figure so what if he stresses me out or beats on me—at least he loves me.

If your man is calling you names or if he hits you, he is not the right guy for you. If your man abuses you physically or emotionally, it's not because he loves you, it's because he's not man enough to channel his anger in a proper way. So he brings it home to wifey.

Even if you have to make do without a man, that's better than being in a stress-filled relationship wondering why he shows his "love" in such a harsh way. I thank God I have never been in a relationship like Beverly's or Jessica's. One reason I think it hasn't happened to me is because my mother brought me up with enough love and self-confidence to know that I am worth loving the right way. I don't believe in settling for less than what I deserve. I was raised by a mother who was always strong and never took crap from any man, and I can't imagine being in a relationship where I was being abused.

If your man abuses you physically or emotionally, it's because he's not man enough to channel his anger in a proper way.

When I meet a guy, I know whether he's immature or violent by the way he talks or presents himself. Once I come to the conclusion he will not be right for me, I usually keep him as an associate or nothing at all.

Yes, I know I sound like a pamphlet or some after-school special, but it's the truth. Saying, "Well my man don't beat on me, he just smacks me around once or twice" is a messed up attitude, and you should learn how to love yourself before you decide to love someone else.

To girls out there who are in relationships like my homegirls Jessica and Bev, get out quick before you find yourself laying in a hospital or worse. And to the ones who are not in those types of relationships, take my advice and never let your man make you feel lower than what you're worth. Peace out and stay strong.

LaTonya was 17 when she wrote this story.

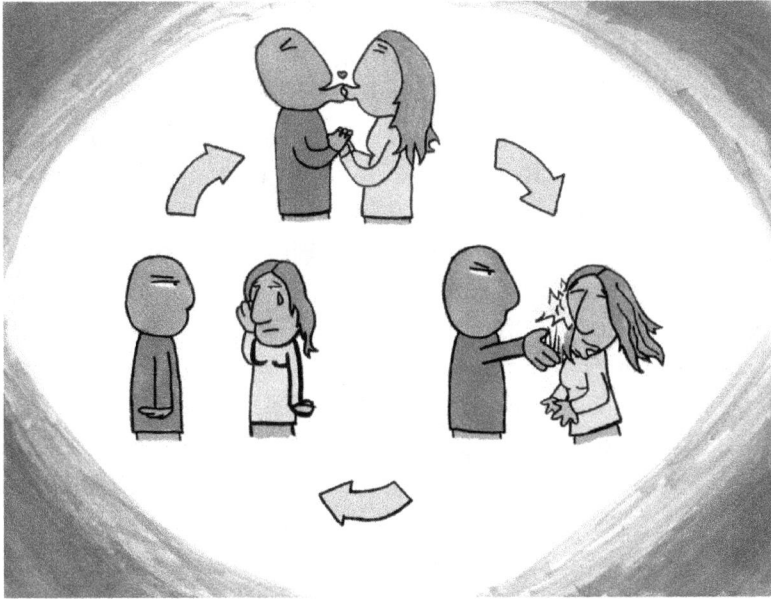

John Morgan

Blinded by Love?

By Anonymous

Recently, I realized I am in an abusive relationship. I have been denying it ever since it started because I didn't want to believe that my boyfriend was a bad person. I didn't want to be seen as a victim.

My boyfriend David and I have been going out for about a year and a half. I met him when he came to play handball with my sister one day. My last boyfriend and I had just broken up and I was looking to be with someone. I felt weak. I didn't want to be alone because I wasn't used to it. I was used to having some-one take care of me.

David liked dancing and Michael Jackson. He wasn't shy and he had a confidence to him. I could tell there was something different about him and I liked that.

When I started going out with David I felt protected and

wanted. I knew that he would keep me safe if any other guy was bothering me. But after a while David started to hit me and I didn't understand why. I don't even remember the first time but it was around 10 months after we started going out. I didn't have a reaction. I just let him hit me because I thought that it was a one-time thing and that he wouldn't keep doing it. But he did.

He never showed any regret. He'd just act like nothing happened. Sometimes when he hit me I'd stop talking to him for a while. I was upset that he would do that to me, but I never thought of him as an abusive guy. I just thought that he had a bad temper. Then I started talking to people about it and they told me that what he was doing wasn't right. I thought about it and I thought, "Maybe they're right and I'm just too blinded by 'love' to see it."

I just let him hit me because I thought that it was a one-time thing and that he wouldn't keep doing it. But he did.

I did some research on abusive relationships. I found out there are things about my relationship that are considered abusive. In an interview I read (you can read it on page 98) it said, "They (abusive men) are very manipulative. Soon they start to control the women's time, putting the women down, or yelling or using physical or verbal violence."

My boyfriend doesn't say nice things to me, and does use some verbal and physical violence. If I see him I have to be on time or he will be mad. He gets jealous easily and sometimes thinks that I'm cheating on him when I'm not.

I read that abuse is not about anger—it's about power and control. This reminded me of David because sometimes after work he'll come home in a bad mood and hit me if I annoy him. If he gets yelled at by his boss he'll wait till he sees me and then take it out on me. It is just that feeling of power that he can do what he wants to me.

According to the interview, people who experienced violence when they were younger are more likely to get into a violent relationship themselves. I'd never heard that before, but it seems true for me. My father was abusive to my mother. He would drink a lot, and then when my mother wouldn't give him any money he'd become violent. I was always afraid of my father and I never felt loved by him. I think that's why, now, I need so much to feel loved and taken care of by men.

The therapist in the interview said there is "a kind of brainwashing that goes on" in abusive relationships, and it makes it hard for the victim to think clearly. "Women are made to feel responsible for the abuse, to feel they caused it and that they don't deserve better, and that if they leave, they are going to get hurt," she said.

Reading that helped me understand why I have stayed with David even though he hits me. When he hits me he usually says it's my fault. I know now that it's not my fault, but I used to think it was.

Once I asked him about another guy that he worked with and he crushed my hand because he got mad that I was asking about someone else. I yelled at him to stop and had a mad look on my face, but he didn't even apologize. Afterwards, I felt a little guilty about asking him about another guy, because he doesn't ever show any interest in any other girl.

Another time, I was at David's house and I was mad that he was going to leave me to go somewhere with his roommate. I didn't know how to tell him I was upset, so I slapped him in the arm and then he went crazy punching me in the leg. I couldn't believe that he got so mad just because I slapped him. I told him, "What the hell is wrong with you? You need to see somebody!"

He said it was my fault because I slapped him first. I shouldn't have slapped him, but he shouldn't have punched me. I don't hurt him and make him cry like he does to me. I asked him, "So you want to be the one in control with all of the power, right?" He said, "Of course!" That showed me that he is not going to change.

Still, I'm not ready to leave him. I've tried a few times. A few months ago I told David I was going to break up with him if he didn't get his act together. But he told me that if I broke up with him he would leave the state. I couldn't believe that he said that because it seemed so drastic. It seemed like he would be so devastated to be without me. And that made me feel sorry for him. I also imagined the pain of being without him and it made me feel so alone that I didn't want to think about it. Even though he was trying to control me, I realized I am still depending on him.

It seemed like he would be so devastated without me, and that made me feel sorry for him.

If I broke up with David, I'm sure I'd miss him and just want to get back together with him. I don't think I can handle being alone. I don't feel comfortable or safe at my foster home and my sister is always busy with college. I don't have too much of a close relationship with my foster mother either.

I feel like the support from my friends and family is not enough. What gets me through the weeks is talking to David every day and knowing that I am going to see him at the end of the week. If I don't have that then I will feel all alone every night.

I still love David, even though sometimes I don't know why. The interview said that therapists can help women sort out their feelings. But I don't feel comfortable talking to a therapist.

I know when he hits me it shouldn't be happening, but he doesn't hit me very often. When I am lying down next to David at night and when we fall asleep I know that he is always going to be there when I wake up. I know that I can talk to him every night and see him every weekend. Right now, that's all that matters.

The author was 19 when she wrote this story.
She went on to attend college.

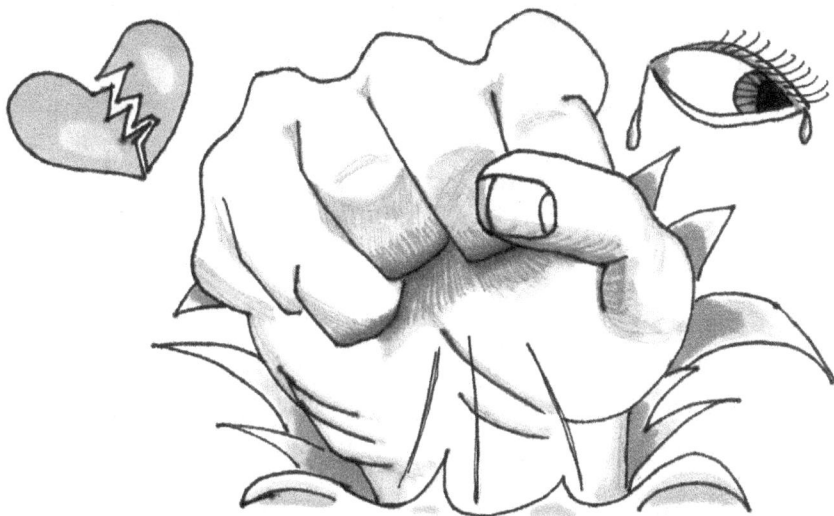

Elizabeth Deegan

Black and Blue

By Zoraida Medina

As I walk up the stairs, I realize what time it is. Early morning. I've just been with Tony, my boyfriend of one month, who my moms doesn't like. She doesn't like him because he's 19 years old and I'm only 12. I'm hoping she won't do anything, but as I get in front of the door, I feel scared.

I knock.

She asks, "Who?"

I say, "It's Sori."

She opens the door. I see the pain in her eyes. She asks, "Where were you at?"

I say, "With my friends." We both know I've really been with my boyfriend.

She says, "Do you realize what time it is?"

"Yes. It's 5 o'clock."

"You know what's gonna happen, right?"

I say, "Yes." I know from the look on her face.

So she tells me to come in and she hits me and keeps on hitting. And as she's hitting we exchange words. Calling each other names. And it's all of a sudden that I feel she shouldn't put her hands on me, and I tell her I'm going to leave. And I mean it. What I don't know is that the person I'm going to leave her for is going to treat me worse, much worse. But that's how it all begins.

For the next three years I was in my mom's house only off and on. I was with Tony the other half of the time. While my moms only hit me to punish me, like when I stayed out all night, Tony hit me whenever he felt the need. Whenever he was mad, he struck me.

When I first saw Tony, he flaunted money in my face and that attracted me. I was coming from the pool with my little brother.

I heard someone say, "Shorty." I looked back because people call me "Sori," and that's what I thought I heard. When I looked at him, he already had the money in his hand, knowing that money attracts little girls. It worked. I saw money, and I saw it to be sweet as candy. That was all I needed to see, and it started from there.

The more my mother told me not to be with him, the more time I spent with him.

From the very beginning, my mother didn't want me with him. She thought I was too young to have a boyfriend and he was too old, but I didn't listen. He was my first boyfriend and I considered myself very grown and bold to be with him, so the more my mother told me not to be with him, the more time I spent with him, even after he started hitting me.

One day I wanted to go to a party and Tony said that I couldn't. I looked at him and said, "Are you bugging?" So he slapped me. That was the first time I stayed out all night with him. I did it just because he told me to. I was kind of worried about how my mother would react with me being gone so long, but I was more worried about what would happen if I said no to Tony.

Over a year went by and things just got worse. I was still with him, living with him now. I was a 14-year-old in a relationship with a 21-year-old. I missed my mother every day that we were away from each other. I needed her, and she was still trying to get me out of the relationship, but now I felt I had no other choice than to stay with Tony. If he hit me for no reason when I was with him, imagine what would happen if I left him. I knew I might end up dead or in a hospital. I didn't want to think about it. And it wasn't just fear that kept me with him—all his hitting and insults made me feel bad about myself, like I couldn't get anyone better than him.

Another year went by. I was going on 15. I stopped going to school because Tony would show up there to harass me. Kept going through it all: beatings, insults, arguments, stress. I got punched, kicked, slapped, slammed against walls, floors, mirrors. He used to call me names, everything he could think of.

We argued for the most stupid reasons, like if I didn't cook or clean. If I came home 20 minutes late he would slap me and then we'd argue. Stress, stress, oh God. And I was tired, so tired. Tired of getting hit. Tired of living the life of someone's slave. Tired of getting followed, of being embarrassed, of being treated like I didn't deserve to set foot on the ground. Tired of smoking weed and cigarettes just to calm myself down.

I truly hated Tony by this point, but I also felt stuck with him. So I learned how to act in ways that wouldn't upset him as much. I acted as if I had no friends, as if the world I was living in was over, and the more I acted like this, the more I started believing it. I felt so ashamed all the time. My relationship with my family was nothing but a whole bunch of regrets.

Tony hit me so bad one day outside, and thank God the cops were there to stop it, 'cause I could've been killed.

Then the cops gave me advice. They told me to get an order of protection on Tony so he couldn't come near me.

Having them tell me to do that helped, because I kept thinking about what they said. The following week I did get the order of protection against Tony.

I had been in and out of my mother's house, running away and coming back for some time. Now I went back to her house for good. My mother was happy about that. She got a lawyer and helped me make my case to him so that the beatings and pain could stop forever.

The day before my 16th birthday, I was with my uncle and aunt when we spotted Tony. He was coming toward me and I told myself I was going to stop running from him. He came to my face talking crap. He said he had a gun, and if I wasn't gonna walk with him he would start shooting. Little did he know that my uncle had gone to call the cops. The cops caught Tony and searched him. They asked me if this was the man I had the order of protection out on. I said, "Yes." They set me a court date for the next day—my birthday.

All his hitting and insults made me feel bad about myself, like I couldn't get anyone better than him.

As I walked into the courthouse, Tony walked in, too. I started crying, I was so scared. Tony had ruled my life for the last several years, all the time I'd been growing up. I'd wanted to kill him so many times and now I was going to testify against him in front of people. I was more than willing to spend my whole birthday in the court because I needed to find my way out of those dark clouds and into the sun where I knew I belonged.

The day I turned 16 years old, at 5 p.m., they found Tony guilty of statutory rape and endangering a minor. I got him locked up.

I felt free from the cages in my mind. I knew I wasn't stuck anymore in a world of hate, lust, and fear. I could finally go back to being myself, alone with my family.

But just because Tony's locked up doesn't mean the pain is over. I'm still scared of him getting out of jail and hurting me. At night I have dreams of him trying to kill me, strangle me, run me over with motorcycles. I'm scared to be alone, without anyone to hold or comfort me. To this day, I jump at any unexpected touch or noise.

It hurts to look back on all those years I was with Tony, that period of pain and anger, of having the desire to kill the man who hurt me every day, of having barely any communication with my mother. I was young and confused and I didn't think before jumping into a relationship. I was 12 going on 13, and didn't know what was good and bad for me, and before I knew it I was stuck. I'm glad, so glad, that I'm not stuck anymore. I still hurt from it, but at least that time is over.

Zoraida was 18 when she wrote this story.

Handel Morency

A Healing Connection:
How therapy can help survivors

Connect and Change, a project run by the Women's Therapy Center Institute in New York City, connects women who have left domestic violence relationships to private practice therapists who provide therapy for free for as long as the women feel they need it.

Many victims of domestic violence join support groups or get short-term counseling. Connect and Change helps women make deeper changes in their lives. Linda Arkin, the program coordinator and a licensed clinical social worker, explains how domestic violence affects women and how they can heal:

Q: How do people get into violent relationships?

A: The truth of the matter is that people get into abusive relationships without realizing it. No one is looking to be abused.

Many women who get into abusive relationships, but definitely not all of them, experienced violence while growing up. If people have witnessed abusive relationships growing up, they have a certain tolerance for violence and are not as quick to realize that what's going on is unacceptable. Sometimes women stay because they keep hoping they can change the abuser, which was something they weren't able to do growing up.

Women also stay because there's an emotional process that takes hold in domestic violence. The victim's thinking changes. To outsiders, it looks like, "Why are they staying?" But there's a kind of brainwashing that goes on that doesn't allow victims to think clearly. Women are made to feel responsible for the abuse, to feel they caused it and that they don't deserve better, and that if they leave they're going to get hurt (which is sometimes true). They're terrified.

Therapists can help women evaluate new partners.

After a while, their ability to test their perceptions against what is really going on is off. "Reality testing" would be, basically, to realize that it's not your fault, it's the abuser's. But your ability to do that has been changed by hearing constant put-downs, and you don't know what's true and what isn't. A lot of what therapists do is to help women realize what's true and what's not true about them, and help them rebuild their sense of self.

Q: How does experiencing domestic violence typically affect women?

A: Women are coming to us because they're out of the relationship but they're still suffering from feelings of sadness or low self-esteem, or they're experiencing effects of violence such as flashbacks, avoidance, or memories of the past that seem to keep coming back.

A feeling of being cut off from your own feelings is very common. A lot of times women have had to really detach emotionally to deal with the situation, and that continues after the relationship is over. You're in a detached state if you're not really dealing with your feelings, or if you're feeling like you don't have any feelings, or if you don't really know what you need or want and are finding it hard to make any decisions.

Someone who is being abused is always walking on eggshells, worrying about the next incident. Life is not about what you need or your children need—it's about what the abuser needs. So you're not asking yourself, "What do I want? What do I need? What do I feel?" It's very hard to make decisions in your life if you don't know what you want, need, or feel.

Q: How can therapy help women heal and stay safe?

A: In therapy, women have a consistent, trustworthy person to talk to about their feelings.

Therapists can help women sort out their feelings as they try to deal with the issues of their lives. Especially if you have children, it's very difficult to get childcare, jobs, apartments, and legal issues taken care of. Therapists can help break down tasks so life feels more manageable.

Therapists can especially help women evaluate new partners. If women haven't taken the time to really understand what happened to them, they can go on to date someone else who will also be violent. It's not that they're looking for an abusive partner, but that their thinking is still off. They're still feeling bad about themselves and unable to make decisions about their own safety. They may downplay safety risks because they feel alone and want the relationship to work.

If you don't get some kind of help—real counseling—to understand the dynamics of abuse, control, and the ways your thinking changes when you're victimized, you're unlikely to choose a different sort of partner.

When people are really conscious of their needs and wants, and understand the cycle of violence, they're likely to spot someone who might be abusive sooner. It's a very conscious effort. You have to become very conscious of yourself and of who you're going out with, so you notice if there's the slightest thing wrong and react to it. If the therapist is hearing about a new guy, and this new partner sounds controlling, the therapist can help with "reality testing."

Sometimes women need a therapist to talk to just to get through the stress of court or the practicalities of daily life, and sometimes they come in depressed and we see that get better as the work goes on. A lot of it is just the therapist helping people get to know themselves. The therapists help them deal with the pain so they can cope with life better.

Originally published in Rise, *a magazine by and for parents involved with the children welfare system.*
www.risemagazine.org

He stood outside her building all day sometimes...

YC Art Dept.

Smarter Than That

By Cheryl Davis

When she was 18, my cousin Renee found what she thought at the time was love. Now 21, she often can't believe the situation she was in was real.

It started innocently. One day when she was getting her nails done at a local salon, Hassan walked by. He tried to call Renee out. She ignored him, but he waited until she came out, determined to get her phone number. Renee thought it was cute. Little did she know, Hassan's persistence that afternoon was just a taste of what lay ahead.

Until I interviewed her, I had no idea what Renee had been put through. We're very close friends, but Renee kept the details of her relationship with Hassan secret for years. As I spoke to her, though, Renee began to open up. "It's very difficult for me to actually speak about this," she said, and she cried a lot while we talked.

To be honest, I didn't want to believe what she said. I felt completely overwhelmed.

Hassan nearly killed Renee more than once. He's dragged her into a back alley, beat her up any number of times, and choked her almost to death.

When he first met her, Hassan showed her the soft and sensitive side that she wanted to see. At first, they had good times together.

"We used to lay down on his bed together and talk about everything. That was our peaceful time," she said. "We used to die laughing and play video games together."

He made Renee feel like he needed her to take care of him. "I wanted someone to love me as strongly as he professed to love me," said Renee. "He loved me and let me take care of him."

At first, Hassan showed her the soft and sensitive side that she wanted to see.

Hassan had been abused as a child, both emotionally and physically. He was beaten for no reason, separated from family members that he loved, and abandoned by his mother shortly before she died.

That's part of why Hassan became extremely jealous of Renee's relationship with her parents, and showed his jealousy in many ways.

"One time he took a picture that I had of me, my little brother and my little sister out of my wallet and he tore it up!" Renee said. "When I got mad about it and tore up a picture that he had of me on his dresser, he got mad and tore up a poem that he wrote me. From there, we had a physical fight."

Later on in the relationship, Hassan admitted to Renee that he felt like her parents were trying to take her away from him. When they said to come home, she would go home.

"He said that he wanted the type of control that my parents had over me," said Renee. "He really didn't understand why it was that I loved my parents, they loved me, and I did what they told me to do. He felt that I loved them more than I loved him."

Hassan tried to make Renee feel guilty, reminding her that she was the only person who cared about him. He always talked about his mother dying when he was young, and stressed how everybody abandoned him and treated him badly. He made her believe that she was all he had.

W hen she tried to leave his side for a moment, Hassan used hitting and cursing as a tool to control Renee.

"He manipulated me and tried to control my every action," she said. He constantly wanted her to be with him, and if she didn't do something that he felt she should do, he would get mad and start arguing with her and end up hitting her.

"When he beat me up, he would not stop until I was crying uncontrollably," she said. "Then he would hold me and cry with me until I stopped."

After they fought, he wouldn't let her leave until they had made up and were on good terms with each other. She had to at least act like she wasn't upset or hurt, because he would become afraid that she would leave him.

It didn't help that Hassan was an alcoholic. When he was drunk, he was even more out of control. "Hassan used to drink so much! Drinking was the first thing that he did when he woke up in the morning," Renee said.

It was hard for me to understand why Renee stayed with Hassan, even though she knew what was in store for her most of the time. She said she was afraid to leave him, and that she wanted to rescue him, to make him better. "I figured he needed me," she said.

As Hassan became more attached, Renee became more detached from her friends and family. He didn't like most of her friends and he wouldn't let Renee hang out with them.

"He didn't like my parents' rules and hated my father especially. He threatened my father to his face a lot and said he would have him killed if he tried to stop us from being together," Renee said.

By then, Renee started to think she wanted everything to stop, but it was too late.

Sometimes, when the violence got unbearable, Renee called the police. Other times, Hassan called them, too, because he was afraid of how out of control he felt.

But she never pressed charges, and the fighting never stopped. Soon, Renee became just as obsessive about Hassan and his whereabouts as he was about her. "I honestly felt as sick as he was sometimes," she said.

She was starting to think that controlling behavior was normal, even though everyone she knew told her it was wrong.

"People who lived along the way would stop me to tell me that they didn't like the way that my boyfriend treated me," Renee said. "I felt like people thought that I was naive or stupid...I was in love."

Eventually, after almost a year, things got so bad that Renee became afraid of Hassan and didn't want to be around him. But it seemed like nothing and no one could keep him away.

Over and over she asked him to leave her alone. She had to hide from him, not answer the phone, not answer the doorbell. She couldn't even go outside. He would call and threaten her family and stand outside her building in any kind of weather or at any time of day.

One cold and wet night, Hassan kept calling her house and hanging the phone up if someone else answered. When she finally picked up the phone, Renee told him that she was not going to come over because it was pouring rain.

Cursing and screaming at her, he said that he wasn't going to stop calling unless she came.

This time, it was Renee who let her anger take control. "I still don't know what came over me. For real, I've never been so angry before," she said. "I left without an umbrella and got to his house in what seemed to be five minutes. I felt like a walking zombie. I wasn't even aware of what was going on around me."

Pushed as far as her anger could go, Renee exploded. "Hassan opened the door with this goofy smile on his face," she said. "I felt like taking his head off! I tried. I punched him as hard as I could in his face."

He punched her back—hard. "To tell you the truth, I didn't feel it until I looked in the mirror in the bathroom. I started screaming on him saying, 'Look what you did to my eye!'" she said.

Hassan then started to cry and say that he was sorry. Renee, now numb to his words, kept right on screaming and let him know that she was tired of his "I'm sorry's" and that it was over, seriously and for good, between them.

When she refused to press charges again, the police officer said, "I thought you were smarter than that."

What Hassan did after that was unbelievable. He got a knife and handed it to Renee, telling her that she had better stab him, because that's the only way that she could ever get rid of him.

Shocked, she stood there trying to figure out where she would end up if she stabbed him. In a mental hospital, or in jail? She was tempted to face whatever was ahead.

"I remember thinking, 'This guy is crazy!' I couldn't believe that this was happening to me," Renee said, in tears. "I was really gonna stab him. I just didn't care no more. He kept tempting me and pushing me to do it. He gave me all sorts of reasons, 'Go ahead, do it! You know you want to! Go ahead! All I do is hurt you anyway! Right? Go ahead!'"

The more he talked, the more she wanted to hurt him like he had always hurt her.

"Just the thought of actually wanting to stab somebody—anybody—was so scary to me. I am not sorry for feeling that way either," Renee said, with rage in her voice.

Finally, she walked out of the bathroom in fear. She put on her jacket and tried to walk out the door, but Hassan grabbed her and wouldn't let her go. Finally, he let her leave because she promised to come back the next day.

When she left, Renee felt numb. Confused, she couldn't tell whether Hassan loved or hated her. She couldn't even figure out if she loved or hated him.

How could he love her if he hit her all the time? How could he love her if he took advantage of her love so much, so often?

That night, everybody in her house ignored her black eye. Renee's mother and father had always told her to break up with Hassan, but they didn't confront her about his abuse.

Later, when they asked her about her black eye, she lied, saying that Hassan's brother threw something at him and it hit her instead.

"I knew that nobody would believe me, but I had to lie out loud since I was already lying to myself," she said.

It wasn't until Hassan tried to beat up Renee in front of her mother that she and her family came to terms with what was going on.

One cold night, Hassan came over drunk. He started ringing the bell, and calling and harassing her. Renee finally went downstairs in some big floppy slippers, a pair of shorts and a T-shirt.

"He got all in my face," she said. "He was telling me how much he loved and missed me and he wanted me to come home with him so we could talk. I told him that we could talk right there in the building."

But he wanted to lay down in his bed and talk with her like they always used to.

She refused to go, but he was not taking no for an answer. He tried to pick her up and put her over his shoulder to carry her out of the building.

"I kept punching him and trying to get away," Renee said.

But he grabbed her by the wrists and dragged her down the steps. "He slammed me into the wall and literally dragged me down the steps by my arm."

Her mom went inside to call the cops. Hassan wouldn't let her go until the police came and pulled him off. He kept saying how much he loved her and needed her. The cops ignored his words and twisted his arm behind his back, slamming him into the wall. Renee sat there thinking about how embarrassed she was.

Once before when Renee called the police on Hassan, she had told the cops that she didn't want to press charges, but that she wasn't going to see Hassan anymore. The police officers that night were really sympathetic to her and very upset with Hassan.

But this time, one of the officers on the scene was the same officer who had been there before. When she refused to press charges again, he looked at her, shook his head and said, "I thought you were smarter than that."

"Those few words are what hurt me the most," Renee said. "That is what really woke me up. I knew he was right."

After the police left, Renee's mother asked her if she wanted to move to Florida with her grandmother to get away for a while.

"I finally broke down like I wanted to and said yes. I knew that that was probably the best thing," said Renee. "I had put my family, myself and even my friends through enough pain. It was time to go."

The week before she left, she hid out in her house. Hassan did not quit trying to see her. He stood outside her building all day sometimes, and kept calling until her mother told him she'd already left.

Renee felt sad about having to leave her family, and disappointed in herself for not listening to her parents' advice sooner. "I was depressed the whole time I was in Florida because I let my whole family down," she said.

You would think by this time Renee would be completely through with Hassan, but it has not been that easy for her. He tracked her down in Florida, and she was too weak to resist talking to him and writing him letters.

Renee says she is partly to blame for what happened because she was never strong enough to leave him, even when she knew he was hurting her in every way.

Even now, she has been broken up with Hassan for two years, but still he is engraved in her heart.

Luckily for Renee, Hassan ended up in jail (for something else completely) so she can't see him anymore. But he has managed to maintain a tight grip on Renee's life.

Deep down, Renee believes she will never stop loving him, even though he treated her so badly. "He changed my whole life," Renee said. "My parents and I do not have the same relationship anymore and I still get scared when someone yells at me."

Renee said she feels afraid of getting into a new relationship, and she's not sure she will ever get over Hassan. Despite all he has done, she said she still loves him, and she believes that he loves her, too.

Cheryl was 17 when she wrote this story.
She later attended college.

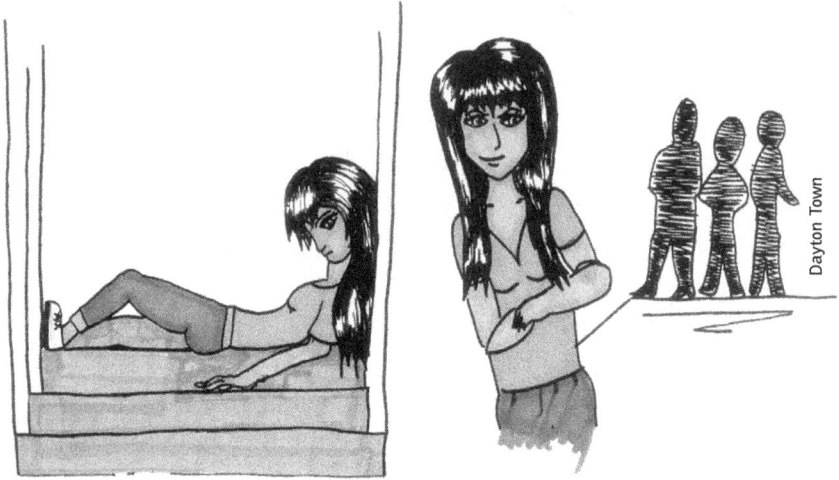

Dayton Town

How to Know if a Relationship Is Good for You

It can be tempting to jump from a bad relationship to a new one that seems better. But how do you know whether to trust a new person? What does a balanced relationship look like? Dr. Karyl McBride is a psychotherapist specializing in treating children who have been abused. She spoke to us about healthy relationships.

Q: What makes a relationship healthy?

A: When you are connecting with someone who brings out the best in you and the relationship is not based on "What can you do for me?" Both people share ideas, feelings, respect. Both people listen and talk, and they do things to help each other.

Empathy, really trying to feel what the other person feels, is a huge piece of a healthy relationship. It's not trying to fix their problem, but just listening to them.

Often adults tell young people what they should be feeling or how to fix the problem. Everybody, including teens, needs someone to hear what they are feeling, because it helps us figure it out. We make better decisions when we know what we are feeling.

In a healthy relationship, you can be your real self. You don't have to act like somebody else to be loved or accepted.

Q: How do you find your real self?

A: By thinking and talking about your own feelings. If you act from your own feelings, you'll be true to your own values. You're not worrying about what other people want you to be or what the media tells you to be.

Q: What questions should you ask yourself about a new relationship?

A: Here are a few:

Is the person able to give and take?

Do you feel valued for who you are rather than what you can do for them?

Can you be yourself?

Can the other person?

Can you have boundaries? Do they respect them? Can you say, "I can't talk now, I have to do my homework," or, "I'm not comfortable telling you that yet"? Or, "I don't want to have sex yet"? You deserve your own space: intellectual space, sexual space, actual physical space, emotional space. And stick to it! Boundaries only work when we enforce them and follow through.

> *In a healthy relationship, you can be your real self. You don't have to act like somebody else to be loved or accepted.*

Q: If you've been abused, how do you know who to trust?

A: The first thing to realize is that you are going to have trust issues, and you're probably going to have them forever. You need to recognize that.

Take it slow with people you don't know. Give them a chance to prove to you that they can be trusted. Don't tell them your whole life story the first time you meet them. You can have boundaries around the pain in your life and you get to choose who you share it with.

If you've been abused, you are going to have trust issues. You need to recognize that.

The more that you learn to trust yourself, the more comfortable you will be in trusting others because your boundaries protect you from people who make you uncomfortable. If we're listening to our inner voice, we will pick up the red flags of another abuser or any other danger.

Q: How can you get help to begin healing and work toward healthy relationships in the future?

A: Getting treatment is very important, because abuse can have long-term effects on your other relationships, including repeating the cycle (being abused again and/or becoming abusive yourself). There are a lot of places that provide therapy for free or at a reduced rate.

Because therapy is so important for working through trauma, ask, ask, ask, until you find the resources you need.

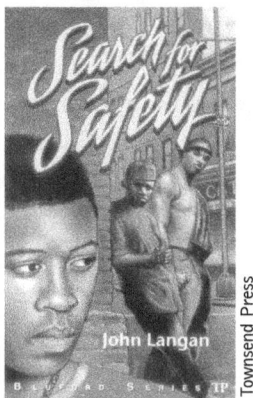

Townsend Press

Search for Safety

"Larry and I are getting married," my mom announced.

We were at the small kitchen table in my Aunt Fay's apartment. My aunt was across from me grading her students' homework. She's an eighth grade teacher who also taught summer school. I was eating pancakes and almost choked when I heard the news.

"*What?!*" Aunt Fay asked, dropping her pen. "You've only been seeing him for a few months. If things are still good after a year or so, *then* marry him. Right now seems too soon, Geneva. You're not pregnant, so why are you rushing?"

Aunt Fay was right. It was too fast.

Larry Taylor and Mom started seeing each other May of my freshman year at Lincoln High School. Now it was only August. During the whole time, Larry hardly said a word to me when he came to pick up my mother. A few times, he gave me a quick handshake, but only when Aunt Fay was watching.

Here's the first chapter from *Search for Safety*, by John Langan, a novel about teens facing difficult situations like the ones you read about in this book. *Search for Safety* is one of several fiction books in the Bluford Series™ by Townsend Press.

"I'm *not* rushing," Mom replied. "Larry thinks it's the right time, and I think it'll be good for me and Ben to be on our own instead of depending on you for everything. Besides, Larry's already found us a place. We're moving in two weeks."

Two weeks. I couldn't believe it. I didn't want to go anywhere. I liked living with Aunt Fay, reading her books and eating stacks of buttery pancakes after church on Sundays with the sun shining right into her living room. It was better than any place Mom and I ever lived in, but I couldn't say that. I couldn't even speak, I was so upset.

Aunt Fay wasn't happy either. She kept shaking her head like she did whenever something bad happened in our neighborhood. I knew why.

Our neighbor Jackie knew Larry from high school. I'd overheard her telling Aunt Fay about him one night back in July. She said people used to call Larry "The Big Hurt" for all the fights he'd gotten into at school.

"*I wouldn't be surprised if he did time somewhere, the things he and his friends used to do,*" Jackie admitted after seeing him pick up my mom one night. "*But that was fifteen long years ago, Fay. People change,*" she had said. Aunt Fay just grunted. They didn't know I was listening.

No matter what anyone said, Mom saw no problems with Larry. She ignored Aunt Fay's advice. Two weeks later, she made me dress up with a shirt and tie like we were going to church. Instead, we went down to the municipal building and got in a line with a bunch of other people. Then an old judge called us into a stuffy conference room, and my mom and Larry were married.

Just like that, I had a stepfather. He didn't look at me the whole time.

The day after the wedding, Mom and I packed our stuff into cardboard boxes and plastic trash bags. Larry came over around noon with a stocky, dark-eyed guy named Donald. Within minutes, they crammed all our things into the back of an old pickup they'd borrowed from somewhere. They left without even saying goodbye to Aunt Fay.

Mom and I followed behind them in Larry's car, and we drove to a rundown row house on Union Street, all the way on the other side of the city. On the way, she dropped another bomb on me.

"You're gonna have to switch to a new school, Ben. It's called Bluford High. Don't worry. Aunt Fay says it's a good school, and Larry says it's no big deal."

What does Larry know? I wanted to say, but I kept my mouth shut as he and Donald quickly unloaded our stuff. They barely talked except when Larry told him what to do or where to put things.

"You get the top floor," Larry grunted to me as I walked into the house for the first time.

He and Donald carried my mattress and old bureau up a narrow stairway that led to the third floor. I followed them, lugging up an old folding chair and a card table.

We entered a small room with a cracked window that faced out onto busy Union Street. The walls were a faded blue, streaked in some places with brown water stains from leaks in the ceiling. A larger back room was empty except for a rusty attic fan mounted in the window. It made a clicking noise when I turned it on and worked only at slow speed.

I spent the rest of the day unpacking and trying to make the dreary room feel like home, but I kept hoping that Mom would change her mind and move back in with Aunt Fay.

It didn't happen.

The next day, I learned Larry's house rules.

It was mid-afternoon, and I was on the couch watching TV when I heard someone unlock the front door. Mom was working her usual shift at the day-care center and wouldn't be back for hours. I figured Larry, a plumber's assistant, had the same schedule. But when he came through the door, I realized I was wrong.

"How's it going?" I mumbled to him. It was our first time alone in the house.

"About time we had a chance to talk," he replied, shouldering past me to the kitchen. He came back a second later with a cold beer and grabbed the TV remote that I'd left on the couch.

"There are gonna be days when your mom and I get back from work and wanna just hang out by ourselves. Maybe Donald and some of our friends will come over too, and we'll need space of our own. We're not gonna want a kid around." he paused to drink some beer. "Now you got a nice room upstairs where you can hang out, and I expect you to use it. You with me, *Benny*?"

Making me leave Aunt Fay and move into the beat-up house was bad, but now Larry was trying to boss me around too. I couldn't keep my mouth shut.

"My mom's paying half the rent here so this is *my* place too," I blurted out. "And my name's Ben, not Benny," I added.

Larry snapped. He slammed down his beer and leaped out of his chair, grabbing me by the shirt. I'm five-eight and weigh 140, but Larry was at least six inches taller than me. His arms were solid like the black metal pipes in Aunt Fay's basement. He held my collar so tight, I almost couldn't breathe. For a second, I was helpless.

Get your hands off me! I wanted to say. But I couldn't speak.

"Don't you ever talk back to me, Bennyboy," he growled. "And if you don't get upstairs and outta my sight right now, you're gonna wish you never met me."

He shoved me against the wall, and I scrambled away from him. Without a word, I raced up the stairs to my room and tried to lock my door to keep him out. But the old door barely fit in its frame, and I had to ram it shut. It seemed crazy to lock myself in the room, but what else could I do? I didn't want Larry anywhere near me.

About an hour later, I heard the front door slam. I looked out my window and saw Larry get in his old Dodge and drive off. It was past lunchtime, and I was hungry. I figured he'd gone back to work and would be out for hours, so I went downstairs to get something to eat.

Aunt Fay had bought us groceries to take with us when we moved, so the kitchen was already stocked with food. First I had a big bowl of corn flakes, and then I made a cheese sandwich. I was pouring myself a glass of orange juice when I heard a car door slam outside. I looked at the clock. It was way too early for Mom to get home.

My stomach sank.

I put my glass down on the counter and darted toward the stairs. I was halfway there when the front door opened. It was Larry. He was carrying a Budweiser twelve-pack. I wanted to get up the steps before he came in, but I wasn't fast enough.

"What are you doing here?!"

Larry's voice boomed through the living room, and his face twisted in anger.

"I just wanted to get something to eat," I said, trying to calm him down. "I'm going back to my room right now." I moved toward the stairs, but Larry stepped in front of me, putting the twelve-pack down.

"When I want you upstairs, you *stay* upstairs!" he yelled.

"But I—"

Whap! Larry cuffed me hard in the jaw with the back of his hand, snapping my head back and splitting my lip. I could taste the blood in my mouth as I stumbled away from him, stunned.

Just get to the stairs, I told myself. I could hear him following me.

I got to the first step when Larry kicked me with his heavy black work boot. The impact slammed against the back of my leg, and I spilled forward on my face, smashing my arms against the hard wooden stairs.

"What are you doing?!" I yelled.

"You're gonna learn to listen to me, one way or the other," he growled, kicking me again in my hip and my backside. I scrambled upward as if my life depended on it. I couldn't believe

I was in this nightmare.

Larry kept coming. I reached the second floor landing, sprinted down the short hallway, and raced up the third-floor steps. But I could hear Larry's heavy footsteps behind me. I managed to shut and lock the door to my room, but Larry was there pounding on it just seconds later.

"Open up, or I'll knock it down!" he yelled. I heard him crash his full weight into the door. The rotting frame began to split and crack. I had no choice but to open it up. Larry stood there, his eyes blazing like a madman's, his heavy fists opening and closing.

I had nowhere to run and no idea what to do. I backed away from him but tripped over my mattress and fell. He stepped forward, his heavy boots just inches from my face. If he kicked me now, he'd break my ribs or worse. I never felt so helpless. I winced, bracing myself for the next impact. But instead of hitting me again, Larry stood over me glaring down.

"I want *respect*, Bennyboy. Don't you ever come down after I tell you to get upstairs. You hear me?" He nudged my shoulder with the thick square toe of his boot.

"I hear you," I said, my voice just above a whisper. He went on about how it was his house but he was cutting me a break this first time. Then he strode out of my room.

When Mom returned home later that afternoon, I could hear her and Larry arguing. Then I heard her climb the stairs to their second-floor bedroom. I knew she was changing out of her work clothes. It's what she always did after she got home. A few minutes later, I heard her flip-flops slapping against the wooden stairs that led to my room. I stayed on the mattress as she walked in and sat down on the folding chair.

"Ben, don't be giving Larry a hard time," she said. "When he gets home from work, he needs time to himself. Just do what he says and stay out of his way."

I looked quickly at my mom and then turned away, my lip still swollen from where he'd backhanded me.

I knew Mom was tired. The weariness in her voice told me she'd had another long day at the daycare center. Maybe someone called out sick, or the kids were acting up again, or a parent got upset about something. I'd heard all the stories she'd told Aunt Fay. And with our move to Union Street, things were harder. Mom's bus ride now was almost an hour long, but I didn't care. None of that made what Larry did right.

"It'll be okay, Ben. Just give him some time," she said. "He's not used to having a kid in the house. I know he'll come around. You'll see."

"But this is our house too," I said, not even looking at her. My eyes started to burn.

"He and I are paying the rent, not you, Ben. You've got to make the best of our situation. We want to make this work."

My heart sank at her words. Mom wasn't going to stand up for me. She'd married Larry, and if push came to shove she was going to take *his* side, not mine.

I closed my eyes and forced the tears back. My mother put her hand on my shoulder, but I shrugged it away. She sighed, frustrated at me. Seconds later I heard the slap of her flip-flops fade as she slowly went down the stairs.

I stared at the ceiling for hours then, watching dark shadows stretch across my room in the dimming sunlight.

They were like the bars of a cage.

Teens:
How to Get More Out of This Book

Self-help: The teens who wrote the stories in this book did so because they hope that telling their stories will help readers who are facing similar challenges. They want you to know that you are not alone, and that taking specific steps can help you manage or overcome very difficult situations. They've done their best to be clear about the actions that worked for them so you can see if they'll work for you.

Writing: You can also use the book to improve your writing skills. Each teen in this book wrote 5-10 drafts of his or her story before it was published. If you read the stories closely you'll see that the teens work to include a beginning, a middle, and an end, and good scenes, description, dialogue, and anecdotes (little stories). To improve your writing, take a look at how these writers construct their stories. Try some of their techniques in your own writing.

Reading: Finally, you'll notice that we include the first chapter from a Bluford Series novel in this book, alongside the true stories by teens. We hope you'll like it enough to continue reading. The more you read, the more you'll strengthen your reading skills. Teens at Youth Communication like the Bluford novels because they explore themes similar to those in their own stories. Your school may already have the Bluford books. If not, you can order them online for only $1.

Resources on the Web

We will occasionally post Think About It questions on our website, www.youthcomm.org, to accompany stories in this and other Youth Communication books. We try out the questions with teens and post the ones they like best. Many teens report that writing answers to those questions in a journal is very helpful.

How to Use This Book in Staff Training

Staff say that reading these stories gives them greater insight into what teens are thinking and feeling, and new strategies for working with them. You can help the staff you work with by using these stories as case studies.

Select one story to read in the group, and ask staff to identify and discuss the main issue facing the teen. There may be disagreement about this, based on the background and experience of staff. That is fine. One point of the exercise is that teens have complex lives and needs. Adults can probably be more effective if they don't focus too narrowly and can see several dimensions of their clients.

Ask staff: What issues or feelings does the story provoke in them? What kind of help do they think the teen wants? What interventions are likely to be most promising? Least effective? Why? How would you build trust with the teen writer? How have other adults failed the teen, and how might that affect his or her willingness to accept help? What other resources would be helpful to this teen, such as peer support, a mentor, counseling, family therapy, etc.

Resources on the Web

From time to time we will post Think About It questions on our website, www.youthcomm.org, to accompany stories in this and other Youth Communication books. We try out the questions with teens and post the ones that they find most effective. We'll also post lesson for some of the stories. Adults can use the questions and lessons in workshops.

Discussion Guide

Teachers and Staff:
How to Use This Book in Groups

When working with teens individually or in groups, you can use these stories can help young people face difficult issues in a way that feels safe to them. That's because talking about the issues in the stories usually feels safer to teens than talking about those same issues in their own lives. Addressing issues through the stories allows for some personal distance; they hit close to home, but not too close. Talking about them opens up a safe place for reflection. As teens gain confidence talking about the issues in the stories, they usually become more comfortable talking about those issues in their own lives.

Below are general questions to guide your discussion. In most cases you can read a story and conduct a discussion in one 45-minute session. Teens are usually happy to read the stories aloud, with each teen reading a paragraph or two. (Allow teens to pass if they don't want to read.) It takes 10-15 minutes to read a story straight through. However, it is often more effective to let workshop participants make comments and discuss the story as you go along. The workshop leader may even want to annotate her copy of the story beforehand with key questions.

If teens read the story ahead of time or silently, it's good to break the ice with a few questions that get everyone on the same page: Who is the main character? How old is she? What happened to her? How did she respond? Another good starting question is: "What stood out for you in the story?" Go around the room and let each person briefly mention one thing.

Then move on to open-ended questions, which encourage participants to think more deeply about what the writers were feeling, the choices they faced, and they actions they took. There are no right or wrong answers to the open-ended questions.

Open-ended questions encourage participants to think about how the themes, emotions and choices in the stories relate to their own lives. Here are some examples of open-ended questions that we have found to be effective. You can use variations of these questions with almost any story in this book.

—What main problem or challenge did the writer face?

—What choices did the teen have in trying to deal with the problem?

—Which way of dealing with the problem was most effective for the teen? Why?

—What strengths, skills, or resources did the teen use to address the challenge?

—If you were in the writer's shoes, what would you have done?

—What could adults have done better to help this young person?

—What have you learned by reading this story that you didn't know before?

—What, if anything, will you do differently after reading this story?

—What surprised you in this story?

—Do you have a different view of this issue, or see a different way of dealing with it, after reading this story? Why or why not?

Credits

The stories in this book originally appeared in the following Youth Communication publications:

"Tearing Our Family Apart," by Jennifer Hoffman, *Represent*, July/August 2007; "Leaving the Bastard," by Merli Desrosier, *Represent*, March/April 2002; "Take Us Away," by Princess Carr, *Represent*, March/April 2002; "How I Escaped: A Parent's Perspective," by Evaliz Andrades, *Rise*, Spring 2007; "Can Men Who Batter Stop?", by Cynthia Orbes, *Represent*, July/August 2007; "Daddy Done Us Wrong," by Anonymous, *New Youth Connections*, November 1995; "Dear Pops: Why'd You Hit Mom?", by Antwaun Garcia, *Represent*, March/April 2002; "Turning Her In," by Anonymous, *Represent*, July/August 2008; "'It's Not Your Fault'", *Represent*, July/August 2007; "Breaking Free," by Anonymous, *Represent*, May/June 2003; "Putting Up With Her Hands," by Derrick B, *Represent*, July/August 2007; "If You Love Me, Don't Hit Me," by Latonya Williams, *Represent*, March/April 1996; "Blinded by Love?", by Anonymous, *Represent*, July/August 2007; "Black and Blue," by Zoraida Medina, *Represent*, May/June 2000; "A Healing Connection," *Rise*, Spring 2007; "Is This Love?", by Cheryl Davis, *New Youth Connections*, January/February 2000; "How to Tell If A Relationship Is Good For You," *Represent*, November/December 2008.

About
Youth Communication

Youth Communication, founded in 1980, is a nonprofit youth development program located in New York City whose mission is to teach writing, journalism, and leadership skills. The teenagers we train become writers for our websites and books and for two print magazines: *New Youth Connections*, a general-interest youth magazine, and *Represent*, a magazine by and for young people in foster care.

Each year, up to 100 young people participate in Youth Communication's school-year and summer journalism workshops, where they work under the direction of full-time professional editors. Most are African American, Latino, or Asian, and many are recent immigrants. The opportunity to reach their peers with accurate portrayals of their lives and important self-help information motivates the young writers to create powerful stories.

Our goal is to run a strong youth development program in which teens produce high quality stories that inform and inspire their peers. Doing so requires us to be sensitive to the complicated lives and emotions of the teen participants while also providing an intellectually rigorous experience. We achieve that goal in the writing/teaching/editing relationship, which is the core of our program.

Our teaching and editorial process begins with discussions

between adult editors and the teen staff. In those meetings, the teens and the editors work together to identify the most important issues in the teens' lives and to figure out how those issues can be turned into stories that will resonate with teen readers.

Once story topics are chosen, students begin the process of crafting their stories. For a personal story, that means revisiting events in one's past to understand their significance for the future. For a commentary, it means developing a logical and persuasive point of view. For a reported story, it means gathering information through research and interviews. Students look inward and outward as they try to make sense of their experiences and the world around them and find the points of intersection between personal and social concerns. That process can take a few weeks or a few months. Stories frequently go through ten or more drafts as students work under the guidance of their editors, the way any professional writer does.

Many of the students who walk through our doors have uneven skills, as a result of poor education, living under extremely stressful conditions, or coming from homes where English is a second language. Yet, to complete their stories, students must successfully perform a wide range of activities, including writing and rewriting, reading, discussion, reflection, research, interviewing, and typing. They must work as members of a team and they must accept individual responsibility. They learn to provide constructive criticism, and to accept it. They engage in explorations of truthfulness, fairness, and accuracy. They meet deadlines. They must develop the audacity to believe that they have something important to say and the humility to recognize that saying it well is not a process of instant gratification. Rather, it usually requires a long, hard struggle through many discussions and much rewriting.

It would be impossible to teach these skills and dispositions as separate, disconnected topics, like grammar, ethics, or assertiveness. However, we find that students make rapid progress when they are learning skills in the context of an inquiry that is personally significant to them and that will benefit their peers.

When teens publish their stories—in *New Youth Connections* and *Represent*, on the web, and in other publications—they reach tens of thousands of teen and adult readers. Teachers, counselors, social workers, and other adults circulate the stories to young people in their classes and out-of-school youth programs. Adults tell us that teens in their programs—including many who are ordinarily resistant to reading—clamor for the stories. Teen readers report that the stories give them information they can't get anywhere else, and inspire them to reflect on their lives and open lines of communication with adults.

Writers usually participate in our program for one semester, though some stay much longer. Years later, many of them report that working here was a turning point in their lives—that it helped them acquire the confidence and skills that they needed for success in college and careers. Scores of our graduates have overcome tremendous obstacles to become journalists, writers, and novelists. They include National Book Award finalist and MacArthur Fellowship winner Edwidge Danticat, novelist Ernesto Quinonez, writer Veronica Chambers, and *New York Times* reporter Rachel Swarns. Hundreds more are working in law, business, and other careers. Many are teachers, principals, and youth workers, and several have started nonprofit youth programs themselves and work as mentors—helping another generation of young people develop their skills and find their voices.

Youth Communication is a nonprofit educational corporation. Contributions are gratefully accepted and are tax deductible to the fullest extent of the law.

To make a contribution, or for information about our publications and programs, including our catalog of over 100 books and curricula for hard-to-reach teens, see www.youthcomm.org

About The Editors

Laura Longhine is the editorial director at Youth Communication, where she oversees editorial work on the organization's books, websites, and magazines. She edited *Represent*, Youth Communication's magazine by and for teens in foster care, for three years.

Prior to joining Youth Communication, Longhine was as a staff writer at the *Free Times*, an alt-weekly in South Carolina, and a freelance reporter for various publications. Her stories have been published in *The New York Times*, *Legal Affairs*, newyorkmetro.com, and *Child Welfare Watch*. She has a bachelor's in English from Tufts University and a master's in journalism from Columbia University.

Longhine is the editor of several other Youth Communication books, including *Watching My Parents Disappear: Teens Write About Living with Drug Addiction* and *Analyze This! A Teen Guide to Therapy and Getting Help*.

Keith Hefner co-founded Youth Communication in 1980 and has directed it ever since. He is the recipient of the Luther P. Jackson Education Award from the New York Association of Black Journalists and a MacArthur Fellowship. He was also a Revson Fellow at Columbia University.

More Helpful Books
From Youth Communication

Do You Have What It Takes? A Comprehensive Guide to Success After Foster Care. In this survival manual, current and former foster teens show how they prepared not only for the practical challenges they've faced on the road to independence, but also the emotional ones. Worksheets and exercises help foster teens plan for their future. Activity pages at the end of each chapter help social workers, independent living instructors, and other leaders use the stories with individuals or in groups. (Youth Communication)

The Struggle to Be Strong: True Stories by Teens About Overcoming Tough Times. Foreword by Veronica Chambers. Help young people identify and build on their own strengths with 30 personal stories about resiliency. (Free Spirit)

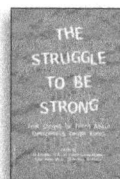

Depression, Anger, Sadness: Teens Write About Facing Difficult Emotions. Give teens the confidence they need to seek help when they need it. These teens write candidly about difficult emotional problems—such as depression, cutting, and domestic violence—and how they have tried to help themselves. (Youth Communication)

What Staff Need to Know: Teens Write About What Works. How can foster parents, group home staff, caseworkers, social workers, and teachers best help teens? These stories show how communication can be improved on both sides, and provide insight into what kinds of approaches and styles work best. (Youth Communication)

Out of the Shadows: Teens Write About Surviving Sexual Abuse. Help teens feel less alone and more hopeful about overcoming the trauma of sexual abuse. This collection includes first-person accounts by male and female survivors grappling with fear, shame, and guilt. (Youth Communication)

Just the Two of Us: Teens Write About Building Good Relationships. Show teens how to make and maintain healthy relationships (and avoid bad ones). Many teens in care have had poor role models and are emotionally vulnerable. These stories demonstrate good and bad choices teens make in friendship and romance. (Youth Communication)

The Fury Inside: Teens Write About Anger. Help teens manage their anger. These writers show how they got better control of their emotions and sought the support of others. (Youth Communication)

Always on the Move: Teens Write About Changing Homes and Staff. Help teens feel less alone with these stories about how their peers have coped with the painful experience of frequent placement changes, and turnover among staff and social workers. (Youth Communication)

Two Moms in My Heart: Teens Write About the Adoption Option. Teens will appreciate these stories by peers who describe how complicated the adoption experience can be—even when it should give them a more stable home than foster care. (Youth Communication)

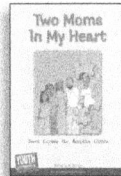

My Secret Addiction: Teens Write About Cutting. These true accounts of cutting, or self-mutilation, offer a window into the personal and family situations that lead to this secret habit, and show how teens can get the help they need. (Youth Communication)

Growing Up Together: Teens Write About Being Parents. Give teens a realistic view of the conflicts and burdens of parenthood with these stories from real teen parents. The stories also reveal how teens grew as individuals by struggling to become responsible parents. (Youth Communication)

To order these and other books, go to:
www.youthcomm.org
or call 212-279-0708 x115

www.ingramcontent.com/pod-product-compliance
Lightning Source LLC
Chambersburg PA
CBHW051732090426
42738CB00010B/2222